The Complete Guide to
Marathon Walking

Dave McGovern
USATF & LSA Certified Coach

World Class Publications
Kingston, NY U.S.A.

Printed by
Southeastern Press, Inc.
258 Glenwood Street
P.O. Box 6127
Mobile, Alabama 36660

Library of Congress cataloging in publication data available.
First Printing July 2000 10 9 8 7 6 5 4 3 2 1
Second Publication June 2005

ISBN 0-9662176-2-4

Cover Photo: Amy Tomlinson
Additional Photography: Monetta Roberts, Amy Tomlinson
Production Coordination: Frank-on-Stein Production, Inc.
Merciless Editing: Monetta Roberts
Research Assistance; Wendy Bumgardner

World Class Publications
P.O. Box 3734
Kingston, NY 12402

Printed in the U.S.A.

DEDICATION

This book is dedicated to anyone who has ever dared to dream big dreams, and to the many people who have helped me to chase mine.

ACKNOWLEDGEMENTS

I would like to thank the Leukemia & Lymphoma Society for getting me back into marathoning; the hosts and participants of my World Class Walking Clinics and Camps for allowing me the privilege of working with them; and my great sponsors, New Balance, PowerBar and Polar Heart Rate Monitors for their unflagging support over the years. Sincerest thanks to my mother, my Aunt Pat, and the rest of my family who continue to encourage me despite my lack of a real job or any discernible direction in life.

FOREWORD

Want to know what this book says? It says if you want to walk a marathon take a bunch of increasingly longer walks on successive weekends, eat plenty of carbohydrates a few days beforehand and during the race, and lube up with Vaseline to avoid blisters and unseemly chafing. That's it—you've got the beef right there. I know this for a fact because the author told me so.

Well, that's basically what Dave McGovern said, when he and I were discussing marathon training programs. I was putting together a training guide for walkers taking part in the Arthritis Foundation's Joints in Motion marathon program (I'm their national "coach"), and comparing notes with Dave on the guidance he provides to walkers in the Leukemia Society's Team in Training marathon program (he's one of their regional coaches). And basically Dave said that's all there is to it: long weekend walks, good nutrition, smart race-day preparation and execution. So, now that you've got it, don't bother reading the rest of the book.

Well, unless you want some inspiration too. You know, a taste of the excitement of training for a 26-mile event, and the thrill of finishing successfully. Because Dave can share lots of that, from experience both as a coach (he's been a top-level coach for most of his adult life) and competitor (he's raced more 20Ks and marathons than he can remember, and even a couple of 50Ks which, based on his body's expungatory response, he'd rather forget). So, if you want some inspiration, read on. But otherwise don't bother.

Unless you'd like a really detailed training program, too. Sure, successively longer weekend walks are the basis, but what do you do the rest of the week? How much longer should the long ones be each weekend? Do you ever rest? When? How much? If you want answers to questions like those—and you should, because they can increase the effectiveness and efficiency of your training immensely—then you should read the book. Otherwise, don't bother.

Unless, of course, you want to avoid the big bonk. You know, hitting the wall—something that walkers can do a lot harder than runners, because you may be out there quite a while. Plenty of time to completely deplete your fuel and suffer a horrible crash—enough to even keep you from finishing the marathon. Of course, Dave offers a lot of insight into eating and hydration during your training, and especially in the final days before the race and during the event itself. Dave had to work through plenty of problems with his own mid-race nutrition (trust me, I know of Dave's "nutritional difficulties" based among other things on the distinct pleasure of having him throw up on my shoes in a 30K race in merciless heat in Venezuela), so he's well equipped to offer battled-tested advice on keeping you body well-fueled and hydrated.

Oh, I suppose you might want to read the book for advice on how to keep yourself healthy and injury-free during the rigors of marathon training, too. I guess the stuff on selecting shoes and gear, planning your race strategy, pacing, getting through "the wall," and recovering from a marathon could even be pretty useful. In fact, if I didn't know better, I'd think maybe Dave was feeding me a line before, and there really is something to training for a marathon. Well, I guess I'll just have to read the book and find out. If you're planning on walking a marathon, I suspect you should, too. And if you aren't sure about it, or even if you've never considered it, read the book anyway. Dave's comprehensive knowledge and infectious enthusiasm is guaranteed to suck you in and have you itching to get your walking shoes on and start training before you're done reading. At the very least you'll learn a ton about turning your walks into real workouts, and have fun doing it.

Good luck in your training—I hope to see you at a marathon soon.

Mark Fenton
Editor at Large,
Walking Magazine

PREFACE

My working title for this book was *Walking a Marathon in 42,195 Easy Steps*. I thought it had a nice ring to it, but everyone said it sounded a little too scary. 42,195 steps, after all, *is* a whole lot of walking. Any way you slice it, a marathon is a marathon, but walking a marathon really is a lot different from running one. If you have enough sense to walk a marathon instead of running it, most of those 42,195 steps really will be relatively *easy* steps.

I started walking marathons in 1986. In those days the New York City Marathon had an elite racewalk division that was usually won by one Olympic or World Champion or another. Somehow I won the thing in 1993 with a pretty fair time of 3:44:05. Being a native New Yorker, I walked the NYCM six or seven times before the elite division was dropped in 1998. After that I never really had the desire to walk another marathon—I mean, how are you going to top New York?

Then Team in Training (TNT) came along. I started co-coaching Mobile Alabama's Leukemia & Lymphoma Society marathon team in 1997. Helping others to reach their goals of walking marathons, and of walking them faster, got me excited about marathoning again. After walking with my TNT charges in the Anchorage, Bermuda, Rock & Roll and Chicago marathons I was bit by the competitive bug. In quick succession between December 1999 and March 2000 I raced—and won—the racewalk divisions of the Honolulu, Mardi Gras and Los Angeles marathons.

Through my many years of competing as a member of the U.S. National Racewalk Team I've had a pretty good idea how to get myself ready for a marathon. But over the past several years, athletes I've coached, and walkers I've met at races have asked me to recommend a good book on marathon walking. And I've always been stumped. There are quite a few very good marathon running books, but I couldn't find a thing on how to *walk* a marathon. And I don't mean there wasn't a *good* book on walking a marathon, I mean there was nothing, good or bad! I kept waiting for one to come along but it never did. So I finally decided to get to work on completing one more marathon—the marathon task of writing and publishing The Complete Guide to Marathon Walking.

It's been a lot of fun, but also a lot of work doing the research for this book—"research" meaning training for and racing a lot of marathons. But if it helps you to get through *your* marathon, it will have been well worth the effort. So best of luck... Train well and race smart, and hopefully we'll see each other at the finish line!

DMcG

CONTENTS

SECTION I

BACKGROUND

Chapter 1

History of the Marathon

According to legend, the first marathon was run by an Athenian soldier named Pheidippides in 490 BC. After the Athenians defeated a Persian army on the plains of Marathon, Pheidippides ran back to Athens, a distance of about 22 miles, to announce the victory. Unfortunately, without the aid of PowerBars, Port-a-Potties, and water stations, he fell dead on the outskirts of the city gasping, "Rejoice, we conquer!" with his last remaining breath.

With such an inauspicious start, it didn't dawn on the Greeks that marathoning could actually be *fun*, so it was centuries before anyone thought of racing long distances for recreation. But in 1896, to commemorate Pheidippides' legendary (although most likely fictitious) run, a marathon was contested in Athens at the first modern Olympic Games, and a sport—*marathoning*—was born.

That first Olympic Marathon, won by 25-year-old Greek shepherd Spiridon Louis in 2:58:50, was approximately 24.8 miles (40 kilometers) long. Until the 1920s, Olympic Marathons were contested at a variety of odd distances from 24.8 miles to 26.5 miles. The marathon distance was finally standardized in 1924—if you can call 26 miles, 385 yards (42.195 kilometers) a standard distance. That rather arbitrary length was first run in the 1908 Olympic Marathon so that the race would start in front of the British Royal Family's reviewing stand at Windsor Castle and finish on the track in London's Olympic Stadium. Nobody really knows why 26.2 miles was eventually selected as the official marathon distance, but it remains the universally recognized standard to this day.

The first marathon boom

The nascent sport was quick to spread beyond the Olympics. The New York City Knickerbocker Athletic Club held the first marathon on U.S. soil on September 20th, 1896, only five months after the Athens Olympics. 24-year-old John McDermott won the race in 3:25:55.

The first non-Olympic marathons in Europe took place two weeks after the New York Knickerbocker event, as 40-kilometer "marathons" were contested in both Hungary and Norway on October 4th, 1896. Other marathons soon followed in France, Denmark, Germany, Sweden and Italy, with many becoming annually contested events.

Beaten to the punch, but not to be outdone, athletes from the Boston Athletic Association who competed at the 1896 Olympic Games in Athens set out to repeat their Olympian feat on their home turf. Boston Athletic Association member and inaugural U.S. Olympic Team Manager John Graham laid out a 24.5-mile route from the Irvington Oval in Boston to Metcalf's Mill in Ashland that closely matched the topography of the original Olympic course.

Just past noon on April 19th, 1897 a 15-member field set out running on the hilly course. Battling blisters, and dodging automobiles in a funeral procession, John McDermott bettered his winning time from the Knickerbocker Marathon by over 30 minutes to win the race. The B.A.A. (Boston) Marathon, which has become an annual—and legendary—event, became for many years the *de facto* world championship in non-Olympic years.

Inspired by the 1904 Olympic Marathon in St. Louis, both Chicago and St. Louis hosted the first editions of annual marathons in 1905. The Yonkers marathon also became an annual event beginning on Thanksgiving Day 1907, and dozens of other amateur and professional marathons were conducted in the northeastern U.S. during the first "marathon boom" of 1907-1909.

Another boom

Marathoning continued to spread throughout the U.S. and around the globe, interrupted only by the difficulties imposed by the World Wars, and to some extent by the Great Depression of the 1930s. But despite continued growth, the sport remained something of a curiosity. Marathons were being contested annually throughout North America,

Europe, Australia, Asia and Africa—not to mention in every edition of the Olympic Games—but even the biggest races had no more than a few hundred entrants well into the 1960s.

And then came Kruschev... Cold War competitiveness with the Eastern Bloc, and the 1961 report by John F. Kennedy's President's Council on Physical Fitness spawned an exercise boom in the United States that helped change Americans' attitudes about running and other forms of exercise. More and more people started running, and more and more of them started running marathons. By the end of the decade participation in established marathons exploded. Where no more than a few hundred runners per year competed at Boston throughout the 1950s and well into the '60s, a record 1,152 toed the line for the start of the 1969 race.

Not surprisingly, there were also more marathons *to* run, as the sport became less of an oddity. 44 marathons were contested in the United States in 1969, compared to only five in 1959—and this was just the beginning of the huge marathon boom of the 1970s and '80s. Marathon opportunities were becoming marvelously plentiful throughout the U.S. and the world—for men.

Women on the run

Although several women ran in marathons from 1896 to the 1960s, for the most part they did so unofficially or in disguise, against the wishes of race organizers and the U.S. and world athletics governing bodies. Then in 1967, Katherine Switzer was officially granted entry in the Boston Marathon—sort of. Women were barred from entering the race but Switzer was mistakenly given a race number when she entered under the name "K. Switzer." After starting the race unnoticed, Switzer was discovered by marathon officials about four miles into the race. Race Director John "Jock" Semple tried to push her off the course but he was sent sprawling by Switzer's 240 lb. hammer-thrower boyfriend, Thomas Miller, who was running the race with her. Although a bit shaken, Switzer finished the race in an unofficial time of 4:20:02.

After her disheartening Boston experience, Switzer spearheaded the movement to change the rules of the Amateur Athletics Union (AAU) and the International Amateur Athletics Federation (IAAF) to allow women to compete officially in Boston and other marathons, and to get a women's marathon included on the Olympic program. The Road

Runners Club of America (RRCA) had long supported women's distance running, but the more conservative AAU feared that marathoning would be harmful to "frail" women.

Boston and Olympic marathon officials continued to resist change, but before long dozens of marathons officially allowed women to enter, including the inaugural New York City Marathon in 1970. Responding to growing pressure, the AAU decided at their 1971 Convention to allow women to compete in races as long as ten miles, and to approve the marathon for "selected women"—which basically meant any woman who had already proven herself by previously finishing a marathon as an "unofficial" entrant. Under continued pressure from race directors, the RRCA, and women's rights groups, the AAU finally changed their bylaws in 1972 to allow women to officially enter marathons. Boston Marathon officials grudgingly caved in to public pressure, allowing women to officially enter the race in 1972, while the AAU conducted their first marathon championship for women in February of 1974. Switzer, backed by the Avon and Nike corporations, continued her fight to get a marathon on the Olympic program. At their annual convention in 1981, the International Olympic Committee (IOC) finally approved women's Olympic 5,000-meter, 10,000-meter and marathon races, clearing the way for women to run those distances at the 1984 Los Angeles Olympics.

With women now permitted to officially enter marathons, and with "jogging" becoming ever more popular in the U.S. and abroad, marathoning was poised for a major breakthrough. Spurred by Frank Shorter's victory in the 1972 Olympic Marathon in Munich and by several best-selling books on the subject, marathoning exploded in the U.S. Charismatic stars like Shorter, Bill Rodgers, Alberto Salazar, Grete Waitz and Joan Benoit Samuelson were also instrumental in popularizing the sport. The New York Marathon grew from a field of 127 runners in 1970 to more than 14,000 in 1980, and to over 25,000 in 1990. Boston, despite strict qualifying time standards, grew to 9,362 entrants in 1990.

And the marathon explosion wasn't confined to the established U.S. races. New marathons throughout the world were growing by leaps and bounds. By 1990, the London, Paris, and Berlin marathons each boasted over 15,000 entrants. Honolulu, Los Angeles, Chicago and Marine Corps also broke the 15,000 mark by 1990.

The "recreational" boom

As impressive as the second marathon boom was, it began to wane by the early 1990s. Participation in most marathons began to level off or even decline. But then there was another groundswell. This wasn't just another bump in numbers, but a change in the demographics and the mindset of the new participants as well. According to marathon historian and *Runner's World* senior writer Hal Higdon, the runners who fueled the boom of the late 1970s and '80s were mainly middle-aged men concerned about their health or physical appearance. They were also concerned about racing to beat their best times and to beat other competitors. But the current marathoning boom is different. As a group, today's marathoners are younger, and more and more of them are females. Most are out there for the pure fun and challenge of it, while many are participating to raise money for a favorite charity. To this new breed of "recreational" marathoners, being a part of an event is more important than beating the clock or other people.

But you—the marathon walker—are responsible for the fastest growing trend in marathoning. Before the 1990s if you walked in a marathon you were seen as something of a failure; you either weren't tough enough or you hadn't trained properly to run the race. In 1982 Cliff Temple wrote in his book *The Marathon Made Easier* "...you could theoretically walk the whole way if you wanted, but that would seem a rather pointless exercise in what is, after all, specifically a running event." Yes, we've certainly come a long way! Today it's perfectly acceptable to walk. Top running coaches like Tom Osler and Jeff Galloway even encourage their runners to take scheduled walking breaks throughout the race, starting in the first few miles. And now more and more marathons have racewalk categories and more and more race directors keep their courses open longer to cater to walkers.

Today's marathon boom is an impressive one. More marathons show up on the calendar every year, and the best races keep getting bigger and better. There are now some 300 marathons held annually throughout the U.S.—at least one in each of the 50 states. And hundreds more are held throughout the world, from the Arctic Circle to Antarctica. Nearly two dozen marathons attract fields of over 10,000 runners and walkers. New events like Orlando's Walt Disney World Marathon, San Diego's Rock & Roll Marathon, and Nashville's Country Music Marathon have attracted huge fields by specifically catering to the new recreational marathon runners and walkers rather than to the elite.

Some long-time runners bemoan the changing face of the marathon, and the "run for fun" (or, God forbid, *walk* for fun!) attitude of today's "recreational" marathoners, but if numbers are any guide, these curmudgeons are definitely in the minority. Recreational marathoning has evolved into a mass participation activity where being a part of a happening is more important than finishing with a fast time. Many races used to stop the clocks and open the roads to traffic after four hours since so few runners finished after that. Nowadays there are far more people who finish marathons with times slower than four hours than there are people finishing faster than four hours.

"Elitist" runners have nothing to fear: Recreational marathon running and walking coexists with and complements more competitive running in the same way that recreational and professional golf coexist with and complement each other. And I've found that for the most part elite runners aren't just tolerant of the growing wave of slower runners and walkers, they welcome them. They understand the commitment it takes for *anyone* to complete a marathon, and they also understand that the masses of non-elite runners and walkers are what attract the sponsors that make their prize money possible.

Marathoning has certainly come a long way from its Athenian roots. What allegedly killed Pheidippides has brought life to hundreds of thousands of runners and walkers who have used the marathon as a way to get and stay fit and healthy. It has grown from a male-only pursuit, to one that now attracts nearly as many women as men. And through the efforts of charity runners and walkers, the marathon has also become a vehicle to save lives—and to improve the quality of life—of millions of people who will never even enter one of the 26.2-mile races.

There's no telling what direction marathoning will take in the 21st century. But if the recent past is any indication, the races will be bigger, better, and more walker-friendly than ever. Who knows, maybe some day marathons will attract 50,000 walkers and will include a special token run category for the few hundred runners who show up! And if that scenario comes to pass, you can look back and say you were a marathon walker back at the turn of the millennium when it all began...

Chapter 2

Why a Marathon?

Every year there are about 500 marathons contested throughout the world—nearly 300 of them in the United States alone. And every year some 800,000 people worldwide complete one of the 26.2-mile races. But even though marathoning is experiencing another boom in popularity, less than .1% of the population has ever attempted, let alone completed one. So any way you slice it, it's still a remarkable undertaking, and a huge accomplishment to have finished the entire 26.2-mile journey. But is that reason enough to put yourself through the rigors of the event—not to mention the months of training that precede it? For most people it very well may be. Finishing a marathon is something you can look back on with pride for the rest of your days. But there are other very good reasons for entering a marathon.

Killing calories

You don't have to be a type-A competitive person to get a huge motivation injection from the marathon. Even non-athletic people who want to maintain a healthy way of life can look to the marathon as a major motivator: an ambitious goal that helps them to stick to a training program. And if your goal is weight loss, there's no better way to burn calories than by training for a 26.2-mile event. Every mile you walk burns a little more than 100 calories. And those walks also build muscle, which helps you to burn even more calories—even after you've finished your workout. You may even find that with all that walking—and the extra time you should spend sleeping to recover from those walks—you'll have difficulty finding the time to eat! In fact, as long as you don't go on major Oreo and Ben & Jerry's binges after your long walks, you'll have a hard time <u>not</u> losing weight!

The final frontier...

Competitive runners and walkers whose times in 5K and 10K races have stopped improving may look to the marathon as the logical next step—a new frontier of sorts. Training for and racing a new distance puts you at the base of the "learning curve," so your first race is guaranteed to be a "personal record"—a PR in runners' lingo. What's more, you're very likely to improve upon that first performance in subsequent marathons as you learn more about training and racing the distance. And as any competitive athlete can tell you, you can't beat a new PR for a big-time motivation boost!

That's not to say you have to be an experienced runner or walker to take the marathon challenge. Most of my Team in Training walkers come to the program without ever having entered a race before. To them the marathon stands alone as a unique life-changing challenge. If you don't currently walk for exercise it may take one or two extra months of base training before you'll be ready to jump into the really long stuff, but with a little patience, you'll get there. And once you do, you'll be ready to embark on an adventure just as thrilling—and life-changing—as receiving your first kiss, getting your driver's license, or writing the Great American Novel. Once you complete the training and cross that marathon finish line you'll no longer be Jane Doe, sedentary key-punch operator, you'll be Jane Doe, Marathoner!

Basic training

If you currently enjoy walking in shorter races, becoming a marathoner-in-training doesn't necessarily mean those days are over. Far from it. The training you'll do for your marathon is a great route to PRs in the shorter races as well. Although 5Ks and 10Ks may be considerably shorter than a marathon, they are by no means sprint events. But many athletes treat them like they are, substituting lots of short, fast road workouts and even shorter, faster speed sessions for more time consuming but much needed longer, slower workouts. Any race that lasts longer than two minutes is primarily an aerobic event, so those long, easy "overdistance" miles are an integral—although often neglected—component of 5K and 10K training.

By training for a marathon, many runners and walkers find that their enhanced endurance results in dramatically improved speed over five or ten kilometers—even if they don't do any specific speed work. Other athletes find that they may slow down a bit in the short races *while* preparing for a marathon, but as soon as they switch back to specific 5K and 10K training, they race these distances faster than they ever had before. Either way, unless you *overtrain*, marathon preparation is great base work for shorter road and track races.

Charity starts on the roads...

If weight loss, endurance-building, increased speed, and taking part in a tradition-rich sporting event aren't reason enough for you, a nobler reason for doing a marathon is to raise money for important charities. In 1986, a New York City Marathon runner whose husband was diagnosed with leukemia passed out pledge forms to family and friends and raised $22,000 for the Leukemia & Lymphoma Society of America. Two years later another runner gathered a group of mostly first-time marathoners to recruit pledges for each mile of the marathon. Together they raised $320,000 for leukemia research. Their success inspired the Leukemia & Lymphoma Society of America to create Team in Training (TNT); a marathon-training program that provides runners and walkers with qualified coaches to help them achieve their goal of finishing a marathon. Each athlete raises funds for the Leukemia & Lymphoma Society in the name of a patient or loved one who is battling or has died from leukemia or related diseases. Participants in the program receive free coaching and mentoring, and a free trip to a world-class marathon like Honolulu, Anchorage, Dublin or London. The benefits of having an experienced coach and the camaraderie that comes from training with other like-minded participants make this a great option for first-time marathoners.

Other charities have followed the Leukemia & Lymphoma Society's lead, with some 15 organizations now fielding teams—the Arthritis Foundation's "Joints in Motion" team, and the American Diabetes Association's "Team Diabetes" being the largest and best known. But there are also marathon training teams dedicated to raising money for, among others, AIDS, pediatric cancer, and multiple sclerosis research.

What's your excuse?

These are all great reasons for entering a marathon. But there are as many good reasons for doing a marathon as there are people who do them. The marathon that you're about to begin training for is your own personal Olympics; your individual Mt. Everest. So you really only need one reason to do it—because it's there!

Probably the best reason for doing a marathon: the feeling you get when it's over! These happy Portland Marathon Walk finishers don't look any worse for the wear after their 26.2-mile journey.

Great Walking Marathons:
Portland Marathon, Portland, OR

The Portland Marathon has long been considered one of the most walker-friendly of all major marathons. The October fixture, the second largest non-prize money marathon in the U.S., has had a well-received marathon walk category since 1989. The field size of some 6,500 runners and walkers is big enough to provide the feel and excitement of an "event" marathon without the claustrophobic crowding of the really big races.

The walk has a separate start from the marathon run, but after the first five blocks, walkers follow the same course as the runners. The relatively flat, fast course takes walkers along the Willamette River, past panoramic views of the Cascade Mountains with Mount Hood and Mount St. Helens in the distance. It crosses the beautiful St. John's suspension bridge, meanders through spectacular tree-lined neighborhoods and historic Old Town. Miles are very well marked with banners, clocks and balloon arches, and the 19 aid stations are manned by enthusiastic volunteers from local businesses and organizations who compete for awards, including best organized, best decorated and most enthusiastic.

Walkers encounter nearly 40 entertainment areas on the course, featuring a wild variety of bands, belly dancers, street performers and clowns. There are even food vendors along the way in case you should have the urge for a hot dog and a beer at 20 miles. A generous 8-hour time limit ensures that all but the slowest competitors have plenty of time to take in the sights and sounds.

Race day weather is almost always good—especially for Portland. The average temperature for the 7:00 a.m. start is 50 degrees, rising to 64 at noon. And believe it or not, it has almost never rained on race day!

Faster walkers compete for racewalk awards, but all finishers receive a long-sleeve T-shirt, finisher's medallion, race pin, Pacific Redwood sapling and a red rose. Race certificates, post-race results, and even Christmas cards are mailed to all finishers. If you're looking for a walker-friendly marathon that strives to make everyone feel like a winner, Portland is the race for you!

Chapter 3

Why Walk?

There's a reason why very few people have ever finished a marathon—it's not easy. But until recently most people set out with the goal of *running* the 26.2-mile race. *Walking* a marathon on the other hand, although certainly not easy, is quite a bit less stressful on the body than running one.

Here's why: If you're like most people, you probably do at least *some* walking every day, which can easily add up to several miles per week. Just think how many miles you walk around the mall while holiday shopping. So most people have developed sufficient muscle and joint strength to allow them to walk for several hours without any specific training, even though they might not be able to run continuously for more than a few minutes.

Running's a pain

Very few marathoners are in it for world records or Olympic medals. In fact, most beginners aren't even worried about their finish times—all they want to do is finish in one piece. But finishing in one piece isn't exactly a sure bet for a marathon runner, especially for a first-time marathon runner. Running a marathon and *training* to run a marathon carry with them fairly high risks of injury—in any given year nearly 50% of all runners will sustain an injury that will alter or stop their training. The human body is simply not "designed" for running such long distances. Sure, with lots of training we can adapt, but we're much better built for either sprinting short distances, or for walking along at an easy pace for very long distances.

So what does that mean? It means your chances of finishing a marathon are a whole lot better if you walk it rather than run it. You may not be able to go as fast in the early miles if you walk, but remember the Tortoise and the Hare? (Hint: the turtle wins.) While you may not *win* the marathon outright, you're sure to beat a whole lot of runners who started out too fast and fell apart, or who wound up getting themselves injured and had to drop out.

The same thing goes for the training leading up to the marathon. If you want to run a marathon, your muscles and joints will have to do a lot of adapting first. With time, they will adapt, but there's a fair chance that you'll sustain at least a few minor injuries along the way before those adaptations occur.

But let's get away from injuries for a minute. Even if you do manage to stay injury-free, running is not an easy or enjoyable thing to do for most beginners. That's because there's not really a "gentle cycle" for the beginning runner. What I mean by that is most untrained people aren't able to run slowly enough to keep their heart rates down in the aerobic zone. So even when they run at a very slow pace, they huff and puff almost immediately. That makes running a great exercise, but it's very difficult to maintain that very high heart rate for hours at a time, so you'll probably have to do a lot of walking during the race anyway. Well, why not just "cut out the middle man" and start out walking right from the start?

Walk the walk

About 67 millions Americans walk for exercise on a regular basis. Of course only a small percentage of them will ever walk a marathon, but they have come to the same conclusion that you have: that walking is the best of all possible forms of exercise. Walking can help control weight, blood sugar and cholesterol levels. It reduces blood pressure and resting heart rate, and can relieve depression, anxiety and stress. It's also a very inexpensive exercise that can be enjoyed anywhere.

Walking is something you do pretty much every day of your life, so your muscles and joints have already adapted to the activity. Consequently, it's easy to do, and there's a relatively low risk of injury. All you have to do to walk a marathon is teach your body to do the same things it already does now, but for a lot longer.

Walking is also a very "scaleable" activity, in that it can take you anywhere from a very, very easy stroll to an extremely vigorous athletic workout. So walking is a great activity for anyone from the most sedentary, out of shape couch potato, to the most competitive athlete. It's also the kind of activity that can take you *from* couch potato to competitive athlete. Competitive racewalker Victoria Herazo began walking for fitness and eventually wound up making the 1992 and 1996 U.S. Olympic Teams.

Sounds like walking is the perfect exercise, doesn't it? It's cheap, low-impact, relatively injury-free and it's a skill that doesn't require years of lessons to develop. So if you decide to walk your marathon instead of running it, chances are very good that you will finish. And that, for most of us, is the point, isn't it? Just like the Olympians, the most important thing is getting yourself to the finish line. Read on to find out the best way to get there...

Chapter 4

Preliminaries

On the first day of our marathon training programs in Mobile, Alabama, my co-coach Monetta Roberts and I tell all the new walkers that, with a strong enough will, any one of them can finish a marathon that day. And I truly believe that. It wouldn't necessarily be easy, and you would be pretty sore or possibly even injured afterwards if you haven't done *any* training, but chances are you would get through all 26.2 miles. Having said that, I also believe that walking a marathon without training for it is a lot like tight-rope walking or belly dancing: Just because you think you can do it, that doesn't necessarily mean that you should.

The decision to walk a marathon should be made in consultation with your coach and your doctor. Walking is one of the safest exercises around, but a marathon is still a major undertaking. Before embarking on this, or any other marathon training program you need to answer one question—just as Dustin Hoffman had to in the movie *Marathon Man*: Is it safe?

If they can do it...

As I'll say over and over in the coming pages, walking a marathon is really not as difficult as you may think. But there may be some conditions that could preclude you from training for one. I just can't think of any... Really, I've tried! Having seen heart patients, leukemia patients, diabetics, 7-year-olds, arthritic octogenarians, double-amputees and even my mother complete marathons, I have a hard time believing that finishing one is as hard as some people make it out to be. I'm 100% convinced that just about anyone who really wants to finish a marathon can, and will.

But, if you are a heart patient, diabetic, or my mother, or if you haven't had a good physical check up in a while, you probably should get a doctor's okay. (Just make sure that doctor isn't the 300 lb. cigar-smoking variety, because he'll no-doubt tell you you're nuts.)

Once you've gotten your doctor's approval to seal your commitment to walk a marathon, you've cleared the most difficult hurdle. After that first step the rest of your steps, as I said in the preface, will be easy ones. Because it's *only* a marathon, and you're up for the challenge. Because...

You're an athlete

That's right, YOU! I know that because you're reading this book. And if you're reading this book, you must want to finish a marathon. And if you want to finish a marathon you will—as long as you decide to walk it! And once you finish a marathon you're a marathoner. And marathoners are athletes. ALL of 'em. So, circular reasoning aside, YOU are an athlete!

Being an athlete isn't so much a physical thing as a mental thing. It's about making those 1,001 little decisions every day that affect your body *and* your mind in very big ways. Will you walk to the store or drive? Take the elevator or walk up the stairs? Choose white or wheat? One lump or two? Paper or plastic? (Huh?)

Every day these and other choices are put before us. Athletes make the right choices. Thinking like an athlete and making the right choices is 90% of *being* an athlete. So *do* make the right choices, but more importantly, go through the thought process and start thinking like a winner.

There's really only one thing that can keep an athlete like you from finishing a marathon, and it's sitting up there between your ears. Convince that blob of gray matter you're going to finish this thing and you will.

Who *should* marathon?

Just about anyone *can* finish a marathon, but who *should* do so? YOU should! Provided you have the desire, and meet the following qualifications:

- You've been walking consistently—3 to 5 days per week—for at least six months. (If you haven't been, now is the time to get started!)

- You are not currently injured or have not recently recovered from a sustained overuse injury.

- You have a doctor's okay to commence training if you smoke or have any problems with weight, respiration (breathing), blood pressure, pulse rate, or cholesterol, or if you've ever been diagnosed with diabetes or heart disease, or if you're over 40.

If you meet those criteria, and you're eager to do something that can change your life in a positive way, you're ready to go. Now take off that belly-dancing costume, and lace up your walking shoes!

Elite Racewalking Division of the 1987 New York City Marathon. Early in the race Ann Jansson of Sweden and Ann Peel of Canada lead Olympic silver medallists Bo Gustafsson of Sweden and Jorge Llopart of Spain; 4-time U.S. Olympians Jim Heiring and Marco Evoniuk; and U.S. National Team members Mark Fenton (now Editor at Large of *Walking Magazine*), Curt Claussen (current American record holder at 50K), Steve Pecinovsky, Mark Bagan, John Slavonic, Mike Stauch, and the author, Dave McGovern, in USA singlet at far right. Gustafsson and Jansson were the eventual male and female winners.

Great Walking Marathons:
New York City Marathon, New York, NY

Throughout the 1980s and early 1990s the New York City Marathon had the best elite racewalking event of any major marathon. Past winners include Olympic Medallists Bo Gustaffson of Sweden, Jorge Llopart of Spain, Carlos Mercenario of Mexico, and Hartwig Gauder and Ronald Weigel of Germany. The elite event was dropped in 1998, but New York remains one of the greatest marathons to walk.

If you survive the tedious pre-race staging in Staten Island, the start on the Verrazano-Narrows Bridge is one of the greatest spectacles in all of sport, with the mayor shooting a howitzer to send some 30,000 athletes out on the extraordinary trek through all five boroughs of New York City. Once over the bridge you enter Brooklyn and encounter the first of the dozens of bands that provide entertainment on the course, and the first members of the cheering throng of some 2 million spectators. The vast majority of the onlookers you'll encounter would offer you the shirts off their backs—or at least some gum, an orange slice, or a swig of their beer—but you'll probably also encounter a fair number of authentic New York wiseacres. But hey, they're usually harmless, their heckling is almost always very witty, and it wouldn't be New York without them, so fuhgeddabowdit!

At 10 hours, New York has one of the most generous time limits around. But you'll probably want to walk a bit faster than that unless a stroll through Central Park after dark is your idea of a good time. Of course with over 30,000 entrants you'll probably never be alone no matter when you finish—and most of the muggers have already learned from previous experience that the people walking with race numbers don't carry wallets!

The New York Marathon is one of the best organized anywhere. The aid stations—both official and unofficial—are top-notch, and the miles are very well marked with clocks, placards and balloon arches. But it's still a very tough course with several steep bridges, a very long gradual rise up 5th Avenue, and lots of nasty hills over the last 4 miles in Central Park. But you know what they say about New York: If you can make it here you can make it anywhere! If you're looking for an exciting race in one of the world's greatest cities, look no further than the New York City Marathon.

Chapter 5

The Poop on Shoes

Inappropriate footwear isn't what ultimately did Pheidippides in, but you'll probably need to wear something a bit more substantial than Greek sandals for your marathon training and racing. Then again, it's easy to go overboard: A lot of so-called "walking" shoes are too stiff and heavy to wear for more than a few miles of easy strolling. If you try to wear these klunky white cowhide "nursing shoes" in a marathon or long training walk you'll end up with hot, sweaty, blistered feet.

According to Spencer White, an athletic industry shoe designer, marathon walkers are much better off wearing lightweight running shoes than the stiff heavy things that most shoe stores sell as walking shoes. But unless you are very overweight or have severe biomechanical problems, the best case, even for "regular" walkers, is to try to find a real live racewalking shoe. Models come and go out of existence often, but the New Balance 100 series (100/110/111) racewalking shoe is one of the better marathon walking shoes I've seen recently. It offers enough support for most walkers to get through the entire marathon safely, and it's lightweight and flexible enough to get you through it comfortably. Assuming they fit right...

Why don't my new shoes fit?

Of all the different things you can look for in a marathon walking shoe, the way it fits *your* foot is the most important consideration. But every foot is different, so it can sometimes be difficult to find shoes that fit your feet properly. The first thing you need to do is forget about the number printed on the shoebox. Your street shoe size may not be anywhere near the size that will work best in a walking shoe. And then there's the wild and wooly world of the athletic shoe industry to contend with... Although the Big Shoe Companies spend millions of dollars on biomechanical research, the initial ideas for most shoes are dreamed up by the marketing people rather than the design team. So, in many cases, shoes are made very differently from the way the biomechanists say they should be because "market research" has shown that these flawed shoes will sell better. Fitness walking shoes are a fine example. Fitness walkers *think* they need a stiff, heavy shoe with a lot of cushioning so that's what the shoe companies sell them, even though biomechanists say walkers would actually be much better off with lighter, more flexible shoes.

When Big Shoe Co., Inc.'s marketing division sends down their wish list, the design team begins drawing up plans. Many new shoe designs are still drawn as flat, 2-dimensional images on paper, but Computer Aided Design (CAD) is becoming more and more the norm. There are literally dozens of pieces that go into even the most basic shoe, so designers tend to specialize within each of about 15 different shoe categories (running, walking, basketball, soccer, cross-training, outdoor, etc.) There are even separate designers working on the upper and the sole of the same shoe.

After the designer draws the shoe, a steel mold is made to shape the foam rubber soles, and patterns are made for each of the pieces that go into the upper. The fabrics for each piece of the upper are then cut and stitched together. Before the shoe is completely stitched it is put on the last—a hard plastic mold that determines the final shape of the shoe.

Each shoe division uses different lasts, although the same last may be used for several different shoes within a particular line. After the upper is completely stitched together, it is sent through a "heat tunnel" (kind of like a smaller version of the automated pizza ovens at Domino's) to set the shape. The completed upper is then cemented to the sole and sent through the heat tunnel again to set the final shape of the finished shoe.

Prototypes are made in men's size 9 and women's size 7, then sent to the wear-testing lab. Shoes are machine-tested for durability, cushioning and other characteristics, and if they make the grade they are sent to athletes for wear testing. Based on athlete reviews, the shoes are then modified and an "extreme size" run is produced (usually size 5 and size 14) to see how the shoes differ in larger and smaller sizes.

If all goes well, a complete size run is produced and then these shoes are sent to athletes for testing. Final modifications, if any, are made to the design based on athlete input, then the designs and prototypes are sent to factories for production.

In theory, the shoes produced by each factory should be identical, but for a variety of reasons shoes can vary widely from their intended size or shape. Factories may run out of a particular fabric and substitute a different material that may stretch or shrink much more than the original, heat and humidity will vary from factory to factory (although most factories are in hot and humid East-Asian countries) which will also alter the shoe, or perhaps a thicker or thinner sock-liner than the design called for will be put into a shoe. These and other factors can cause a shoe to be as much as 1½ sizes larger or smaller than the size printed on the shoe—which can obviously be very frustrating.

This is well beyond the point where you should be asking yourself: "Self? What's Dave getting at?" Well, what I'm getting at is that just as in any other complicated process, there are a lot of places in the shoemaking process where things can get goofed up. So whether you're buying a Rolls Royce or a new pair of walking shoes, sometimes you can get stuck with a lemon.

Make sure your shoes fit properly before buying them no matter what number is printed on the box or label—even if you've already owned and been satisfied with a pair of the same shoes. Another point is that a lot of what goes on in a major shoe company is market driven rather than common sense driven. Marketers figure a "new and improved" version of a shoe will sell better so they change shoe designs constantly. When you find a shoe model you're happy with, buy several pair, because they're inevitably going to stop making your "perfect shoe."

What to look for in a shoe (besides your old socks)

It's not completely hopeless. Just about every major athletic shoe manufacturer makes at least a few walking or running shoe models that are suitable for marathon walking. And several manufacturers, including New Balance, Reebok and adidas make, or have recently made, racewalking shoes. To keep your feet happy and healthy, look for the following in your marathon shoes:

- **Flexibility.** Both in the forefoot and medially (side-to-side). Your shoes must be flexible enough to allow your feet to "roll" from heel to toe when you walk. If the shoe is too stiff to flex a bit from the middle of the shoe to the toe, and a bit from side to side, you'll be a very "stumpy" walker. You'll also end up with sore shins when your feet slap down on the ground instead of gracefully rolling along as they will in more flexible shoes.

- **A relatively low heel.** Strange but true: The more cushioning you have in a shoe, the harder you'll hit the ground when you walk. Huh? It's like this: The foot acts like a lever, with the ankle as the fulcrum. The bigger the heel on the shoe, the more force you will have acting on this lever, forcing your foot to flatten out upon heel-strike. With a low heel your feet will roll very easily along the ground.

- **A wide toe box.** Make sure there's plenty of "wiggle room" for your toes to spread out when you walk. Cramped toes will become blistered toes, and you'll probably wind up with a black toenail or two once you start your longer walks.

- **Keep it light.** Racewalking shoes, lightweight walking shoes, or running "road flats" are the answer. If buying running shoes, look for something designed for racing 15Ks to marathons, rather than sprint or cross-country flats, which offer little support. The shoes should be lightweight, low profile and flexible, with a breathable upper and a relatively low heel.

- **Buy 'em big.** If in doubt, buy shoes the next half size up. You land on your heel, then roll forward when walking, so your heel stays pressed up against the back of the shoe. That means your foot won't slip as much as a runner's will, so you may be able to get away with a shoe that's a bit large, but a shoe that's too small will give you blisters and black toenails. Besides, your feet will swell when you walk—especially when you walk 26.2 miles. So shoes that are a "perfect fit" in the store may be too tight once you take them out for a long walk.

Inserts

If you have shin, knee or lower back pain when you walk you might want to consider shoe inserts. Inserts are designed to keep your feet in the proper position when you walk, and to give them better support and cushioning than you'll get from the flimsy "sock liner" that most shoes come with. I use a simple $6 pair of Dr. Scholl's arch supports, but you can buy more expensive, specially designed runners' shoe inserts at specialty running and walking stores. I'm just not sure they're any better than the cheaper drug store version.

Orthotics are another option if you have persistent problems that don't clear up with a cheaper support. Orthotics are inserts that are custom-molded to your feet by a podiatrist or orthopedist. They can be effective, but at about $150 or more per pair I'd certainly consider them a last resort.

Where to get them

Rule #1 in buying a walking shoe: The pimply-faced kid in the mall shoe store doesn't care about you or your marathon, and he is *always* going to sell you the wrong shoes. Since 90% of athletic shoes are bought by kids who are trying to look cool rather than by real athletes like you, the majority of "athletic" shoe stores don't sell anything for people who'll actually use them for athletic pursuits. If you want to spend $69.99 or more for black toenails, blood blisters and sore shins, go ahead, but don't say I didn't warn you.

Your best bet is to find a specialty running and/or walking store—and even then you may have to educate the salespeople about what attributes you need in a marathon walking shoe. Once you do find a pair of shoes that works for you, try them out for a few days at home. If you still love them after a couple of workouts, go back and buy two or three pair, since shoe companies frequently "upgrade" their shoes which almost always results in a "new and improved" model that's totally unusable. You might be able to find a better price from one of the mail-order catalogs or internet shoe sites, but get your first pair at a specialty store so you'll be sure they're the right shoes and the right fit for you. If you feel you're ready to go to catalogs, Hoys, Eastbay, and Road Runner Sports are all reputable companies with a good selection of racing flats and racewalking shoes.

The "Shoe Deals" section of my web site (www.surf.to/worldclass) is a good place to start your navigation. Whenever I find a great price on a good walking shoe I put a link to the web site on my deals page. You can usually find bargains on new shoes at these sites, but you can do even better if you don't mind being "out of fashion" since many stores sell their end of season stock at drastically reduced prices.

You may also be able to land some good shoes for free by "wear testing." The major shoe companies need to test their new shoe lines on real people. The initial run is usually in men's size 9 and women's size 7, but later trials go to extreme sizes like 5 and 14, and then to a complete size run right before production. You'll have to send the shoes back after six or eight weeks, but if you're the right size you may be able to get quite a few pairs of new shoes out of the deal. Give the big shoe companies a call to get on their lists: New Balance (800) 622-1218; Nike (800) 344-6453; Reebok (888) 898-9028; adidas (503) 972-2300.

Getting the Perfect Fit

Wherever you get your shoes, remember that fit is more important than fashion. When trying on new shoes, wear the same socks as well as any shoe inserts or orthotics you will wear in training or racing. Also, remember that your feet swell during the day, so try on shoes late in the day—preferably after a workout—when your feet are largest. And don't be afraid to walk around a bit in the store, or on carpet at home, to make sure the shoes fit in action.

Also, make sure you break your new shoes in slowly. A good, lightweight walking shoe won't need nearly as much break-in time as a stiff, klunky leather one, but it's never a good idea to try out a brand new pair of shoes in a race or very long workout. Try them out for three or four miles first, then build up from there. After you've put about 50 miles on them, including at least one 15- to 20-mile walk, your shoes should be safe to wear during a marathon. You can expect to get 400 to 500 miles out of a good pair of marathon training shoes, but don't put more than 200 miles on your marathon racing shoes before the marathon. You want your racers to be broken in, not broken down!

Always train with at least two pair of shoes in rotation, since shoes don't break down as quickly when they are permitted to "rebound" for 48 hours between wearings. Alternating shoes will also ensure that you'll always have a dry pair of shoes to wear when the conditions have been wet, or sweltering—I know my shoes are as wet after I've sweated in them on a hot and humid day as they are after a good rain storm!

Walking is one of the cheapest fitness or athletic pursuits imaginable. It's okay to look for bargains, but make sure the shoes you end up with are the right ones for *your* feet. Because 20 miles into a marathon is a really terrible place to experience the "agony of da feet."

Chapter 6

Fundraising

Since so many people who decide to walk a marathon do so as part of a charity group, I thought it would be important to devote a few words to fundraising.

Most charity marathoners have a fundraising goal of between $2,000 and $5,000. A small part of the money they raise—generally no more than 25%—goes towards their airfare, lodging, entry fee for the marathon, and administrative expenses. The rest goes to the charity. Very few people have the resources available to cut a check for that much money, so they need to involve themselves in fundraising activities.

The problem is, the majority of walkers who sign up for a charity marathon haven't thought about fundraising since their junior high school bake sale, car wash or Girl Scout cookie days—and let me tell you, $5,000 is a whole heck of a lot of pecan sandies. To raise that kind of money, you need to have the right outlook, you need a plan, and you need to be creative.

Attitude adjustment

Before starting your fundraising program, it's a good idea to examine your own beliefs about asking people to contribute money. A lot of people feel embarrassed or guilty about asking others for money—I know I do! But you're really not doing this for yourself. If you wanted to make $3,000 for yourself it would be a lot easier and more profitable to work the fry vat at Burger King for 16 or 20 weeks than it would be to train and raise funds to walk a marathon for the same period of time.

You're walking your marathon to raise money for an important cause, and the people you ask for help know that. The worst thing they can do is say they can't help. But the worst thing *you* can do is not ask. For starters, you never know who has been touched by the charity for which you are fundraising. The Leukemia & Lymphoma Society "Team in Training" walkers I coach are always amazed by the letters they get back from people they've asked for money. The "poor" auto mechanic that you decide not to ask may have lost a loved one to leukemia, diabetes, AIDS, or whichever charity you're raising funds for. Not everyone can write you a big check, but a lot of the people you least expect to come through will want to help you in any way they can.

You may even run the risk of offending people you didn't ask. If you asked all of your friends to help your cause except for one who you thought couldn't afford to help you, how is she going to feel? Like a second-class citizen, that's how! Don't risk offending anyone by not asking them for a donation.

Letter writing

This is the most tried-and-true way to raise funds, particularly for first-time fundraisers. Quality and quantity are what count: Write a great letter and send it to as many people as you possibly can. Professional fundraisers recommend sending letters to at least 150 potential donors, including friends, family, and anyone you regularly give money to—your doctor, veterinarian or hairdresser, for example. And carry copies of your letter everywhere you go. You never know who you'll run into at the supermarket or gas station.

Your letter should be personal, but keep it short—no more than one page. It's easy to get carried away when writing about a cause you care deeply about, but very few people will take the time to read a four- or five-page missive.

One of the most effective letters I've read was all of two lines. It read:

Dear Friends;

I'm walking a marathon to help children with Leukemia.
You know the drill.

Please send checks to:

followed by the writer's name and address. Of course you can add a little more information than that, but be sure to get right to the point.

Be creative

Although you should be able to meet most of your fundraising goal through your letter writing campaign, many walkers have been wildly successful with other activities like raffles or auctions. Some ideas that have worked for my charity marathoners:

- **Set up a raffle.** A raffle is a great option if you have friends in local businesses who would be willing to donate merchandise. You may even be able to find a local printer to donate the printing of the raffle tickets.

- **Throw a party.** I know a number of walkers who have been very successful selling tickets to wine and cheese parties, barbecues or "keggers." Many have also held **silent auctions** at their parties. Merchandise is donated by local businesses, and participants write out bids to purchase the items or services. The highest bid wins, and your charity gets to keep the proceeds.

- **Raffle or auction a day off.** Get your boss to donate a free personal or vacation day to the highest bidder, or to the winner of a $5 to $10 per ticket raffle. The great thing about this idea is that it doesn't cost the company much and it's great PR for them.

- **Have a treadmill marathon.** This is a great way to kill two birds with one stone. You can get in one of your long walks *and* have people pay you for it! Set up a treadmill in a public place like a health club or shopping mall and walk for donations, either by yourself, or relaying with one or two other participants.

- **Have a garage sale.** Another great way to kill a couple of birds. You get to clean out a lot of clutter in your house, and you raise money for your marathon. One of our marathoners was even able to convince her friends to donate their old golf clubs, books, and records for her yard sale. Some walkers even visit their neighbors' yard sales and convince the sellers to donate anything that they can't sell themselves.

Corporate fundraising

Every first-time fundraiser comes up with the same brilliant plan independently: "I know! I'll write to Nike [substitute Bill Gates or another Corporate Giant of your choice] and ask them to sponsor me—when they hear my story they'll write me a $3,000 check from petty cash on the spot!" I hate to be the one to burst your bubble, but it ain't gonna happen. That's not to say corporations won't help you. It's just not as easy as writing to a mega-buck company that you have no ties to and asking them for a donation, that's all.

Many companies do have budgets set up specifically for charity donation. If you work for such a corporation you may simply have to ask human resources for the appropriate paperwork to receive a sizeable contribution. In return, your charity will most likely print the corporation's logo on the team members' race singlets (racing tops), which is a good selling point when approaching the company.

If you don't work for such a business, but you have friends or family that do, have them pitch your request to their human resources departments. Even if your friends or family aren't the ones in need of sponsorship, their connection to the company will be more likely to loosen the purse strings than would a request from somebody with no connection to the company.

Many corporations or businesses will also *match* funds raised or donated by their employees. To find out if your company matches funds, and what their policy is, speak to your human resources department. If you don't work for a fund-matching company, consider contacting local merchants about conducting a fundraiser on their property. Many Wal-Marts and Sam's Clubs will match charity donations raised on site.

Do it NOW!

Whatever approach you take, don't procrastinate. The time to start writing letters or approaching your companies for donations is NOW! It can often take several weeks for a request to get through a corporation's red tape mill, and individuals you ask for money are probably just as good at procrastinating as you are. Getting your letters out as soon as you join the charity team will give you time to send a follow-up letter if the response to your first one isn't what you had hoped it would be. If you wait too long to get your first letter out you won't have the option of a follow-up. Fundraising might not be the most enjoyable thing you've ever done, but with the right approach it can be relatively painless. And it's a win-win proposition: You're helping your favorite charity to raise money, and you get yourself a free trip to your marathon without having to worry about any logistical problems like booking flights or hotels. The best part is that the money *is* out there. And with a little persistence or patience there's no doubt you'll find it.

Mollie Batley on:
Fundraising Tips

Age: 36
Fundraising Goal: $25,000
Marathons Completed: Rock & Roll '00, '01.

Molly and her husband J.J. have three children, Shelton, ten; Shelby, seven; and Ann Marie, four. At age four, Shelby was diagnosed with leukemia. So Molly signed up to walk the Rock & Roll Marathon with her local Leukemia & Lymphoma Society "Team in Training" chapter and set out to raise as much money as she could to help fight the disease. With no help from corporate sponsors, she raised over $28,000.

Mollie says: "When I found out Shelby had leukemia I felt completely helpless. Then I was contacted by the Leukemia Society about signing Shelby up as a patient honoree. After talking with the Leukemia Society team leader I realized I could walk the marathon too. I became extremely excited because I finally felt I could take some control of the disease. I started training and thinking of ways I could raise money.

"As soon as people heard about what I was doing, the money started rolling in. Before I had even sent out my fundraising letter in the mail, I had raised almost $2,000. That was just from word of mouth and e-mail. I have a passion [for fundraising] that I am aware most people don't have, but I think the most important thing that any charity marathon fundraiser has to do is to get to know their patient honoree. That will make your mission more personal, and from there I believe the passion will come.

"Most walkers use letter-writing as their primary fundraiser. Your passion and the connection to your honoree will help you to write a great letter. Then you need to get out your address book and holiday card list and send copies to *everybody*. Start with friends, family and co-workers, but also send copies to anyone you've ever given money to, from doctors, dentists and veterinarians to hairdressers, termite inspectors and piano tuners. Don't leave anyone out, because you really never know who will send you a check. And include a self-addressed stamped envelope with each letter to make it easier for your potential donors to pop a check in the mail."

SECTION II

TRAINING

Chapter 7

Technique

*H*ow you walk your marathon has a lot to do with *how fast* you'll walk your marathon. Walking the way you learned to do it back when you were still waddling around in Pampers is guaranteed to get you from point A to point B—as long as you don't need to get there in a hurry. If your goal is simply to finish a marathon, "regular" walking in a way that feels comfortable and natural to you is probably your best bet. But if you want to get there a little faster you may want to consider *racewalking*, or at least adding some elements of racewalking technique to your walking gait.

Racewalking?

Racewalking, an Olympic event since 1908, is a technique that allows a good walker to finish a marathon in less than four hours by maximizing the efficiency of the natural walking motion. There are specific rules that racewalkers have to follow in judged racewalking events, but for our purposes we just want to borrow some of the elements that make racewalking technique so fast and efficient without necessarily adhering strictly to the rules of the sport.

Most "regular" walkers tend to take longer and longer strides as they try to increase their speed (Figure 1A). But racewalkers have learned that taking long strides in front of the body is horribly inefficient. As your heel strikes the ground in front of you when you fitness walk, leverage causes the foot to flatten out. And that flat foot acts just like a brake, slowing your forward momentum in the same way that landing flat-footed brakes your momentum when you cut from side to side while playing tennis or basketball. Pushing your whole body up and over that long front leg and flattened foot takes a lot of unnecessary energy. Racewalkers take much shorter strides in front of their bodies, so they roll very easily over their front feet and legs (Figure 1B).

37

Figure 1.

A   **B**

Photo A shows an inefficient, overstriding walker whose heel lands far in front of a vertical line dropped down from the center of gravity (C.G.). The heel strikes the ground at a very sharp angle, which causes the foot to "flatten out." just after heel contact. A flat foot in front of the body "puts the brakes on" forward momentum. Photo B shows the heel landing very close to C.G., and the front leg almost vertical, making it much easier to "get over" the leg. Since the heel contacts the ground at a much lower angle there is less force tending to "flatten out" the foot, allowing a smooth "rolling" motion to occur. At heel contact, walker B has about 70% of the stride pushing from behind the body, and only 30% in front compared to walker A's inefficient 50/50 posture. Walker A also walks with the arms fully extended, while walker B bends the elbows. Bending the elbows helps walker B to achieve shorter, faster strides.

To further increase speed, a racewalker tries to maximize both stride frequency (cadence) and stride length. The secret is that racewalkers will maximize stride length *behind* the body. That way the long stride doesn't get in the way of a fast cadence rate. One of the keys to increasing both stride length and foot speed is the arms. Walking with your arms swinging fully extended, like two long pendulums, causes a very long, slow stride. By bending your elbows to about 90 degrees you'll walk with much faster, more powerful strides.

Spin your wheels

You may have to sacrifice stride length a bit at first to achieve a high turnover rate. Don't worry about it. Efficient walking is a lot like "spinning" in a high gear on a bicycle: With a shorter stride it's much easier to achieve a high stride frequency because there is less resistance to overcome. In the end, you'll wind up moving forward faster and with less effort.

Counting your strides every once in a while is a good way to make sure your new, quicker technique isn't getting sloppy. Count every other footfall for 15 seconds, then multiply by eight to determine your strides per minute. There's no "right answer," but a stride count over 140 or so is a pretty good clip. A good racewalker will be closer to 180 or more. If you fall towards the low end of the range, work on shortening your stride. Counting your strides, or at least being aware of the sound of your footfalls, will not only help your technique, it can also help you to gauge your walking pace. After putting in many miles of training for your marathon you'll begin to learn the "feel" of your various training and racing paces, from your easiest recovery day pace to marathon race pace and beyond.

The value of an efficient walking stride can't be overstated. But reading about walking efficiently and doing it are two entirely different things. So how do you learn to take those quick, efficient steps?

Use your feet

The first "step" is to simply do it: Just take quicker steps. But there are other ways to add more power to each step, and using your feet is one of the best. Your feet are the only parts of your body in contact with the ground when you walk. An obvious point perhaps, but one that is often overlooked. The feet should be an active part of the walking motion, but the first thing you need to do is keep them out of your way. The foot should roll like a wheel or a rocking chair rocker from heel to toe as the body pivots over the lead leg. If the muscles of the foot and the lower leg are weak, the force of the ground acting on the back part of the shoe will cause the foot to "flatten out" prematurely. Overstriding will tend to cause an even more pronounced "flattening," since the heel strikes the ground at a sharper angle. Having that flat foot out in front of you will slow you down by preventing you from rolling forward easily over your front leg. Big, heavy, inflexible, "klunky" shoes will also exacerbate "flattening," barring a smooth rolling motion.

Keeping your feet out of the way at the front of the stride is critical, but it's equally important to *use* the feet for propulsion and stride lengthening at the back of the stride. Forward propulsion comes from pushing the rear leg *back* against the ground, which creates leverage that vaults you forward. Keeping the rear foot on the ground as long as possible by rolling up onto the toe at push-off (Figure 2B) will maximize leverage.

Figure 2.

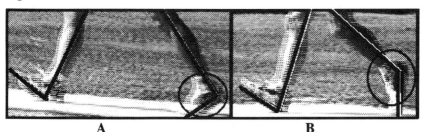

A   B

Walker A. is walking inefficiently. The feet are very inactive, pushing off very little behind the body, and landing very far in front of the body which will cause them to "flatten out" prematurely. Walker B, racewalking, uses the feet for propulsion. The rear foot opens up in relation to the shin, as the walker rolls off the tips of the toes. The front foot doesn't flatten prematurely, so the walker can roll very easily over the foot.

Using your feet more and adding other elements of racewalking technique to your walking style may feel a little strange at first, but if you give it a chance your new stride will quickly start to feel very natural. And once it does you just might find yourself walking faster and more smoothly than you ever thought possible. If you want to take your walking to the next level, head to www.walkertownusa.com to find a racewalking club in your area.

Mixing It Up

You don't necessarily have to become a full-time racewalker to reap the benefits of the faster, more efficient technique, and possibly make a big improvement in your marathon times. I've had a lot of success teaching all of my marathon walkers racewalking technique so they can throw in short bursts every mile or so in their marathons.

Without putting in a lot of miles using the new technique, they can't maintain it for very long during the race, but many walkers are able to go from a 15- or 16-minute mile pace to a 12-minute mile pace or faster for a few minutes at a time. Doing so enables them to give their "regular" walking muscles a break, while moving at a much faster pace. Using this "secret weapon" can lead to improvements of 30 minutes or more in your marathon time. And anything that can do that is certainly worth a try!

Putting it together

Whether you decide to try racewalking or not (and if you do want to try racewalking, www.racewalking.org is a great place to start...) the following technique tips will help you to complete your marathon faster and easier:

- **Relax!** Hey, it's only a marathon. Try to avoid carrying tension in your neck and shoulders, don't clench your fists, and *think* relaxed technique, and you'll walk faster with less energy.

- **Walk tall.** Keep your head up and maintain good posture to keep tension out of your neck and shoulders. Look ahead 10 to 20 feet, and don't bend forward at the waist. Good posture is easier on your lower back, and allows you to take deeper breaths.

- **Keep it short and sweet.** Don't take long, slow strides. Shorter, faster steps are less tiring than longer, slower ones. Short, rolling strides are also a lot easier on your knees, hips and lower back than long ones.

- **Bend your elbows.** Most fitness walkers walk with long, slow inefficient strides. Racewalkers and good marathon walkers use shorter, faster, more efficient strides. Bending your elbows at a 90- to 100-degree angle will help you to spin your wheels quickly. Try to keep your arms swinging close to your sides instead of "chicken winging" your elbows out.

- **Use your feet.** Try to roll gracefully from heel to toe on your feet rather than slapping down flat-footed. Also, *use* your feet. Push off your toes at the end of your stride to increase your stride length.

41

What about hills?

Like death and taxes... Over the span of 26 miles it's almost impossible to not come across at least some hills on a marathon course. Even the flattest marathons usually have some arched bridges to cross. So it's important to know how to handle them.

For starters, you shouldn't change your technique drastically on a hill, up or down. When going up you'll have to cut your stride a bit since the hill is rising in front of you. You'll probably also have to pump your arms a bit more vigorously. But you should maintain your erect posture, continue using your feet, and work very hard at staying relaxed—if that's not too much of an oxymoron. Same thing when going downhill: no drastic changes. Drop your arms a little lower to keep your center of gravity low, and perhaps lengthen your stride a bit in front of your body to brake yourself if it's a steep hill, but otherwise your technique should be as relaxed and efficient as it is on the flats.

A marathon is a long way to walk. Rolling through those miles with smooth, efficient technique will get you to the finish line faster and with less strain on your muscles and joints. If you make no other changes to your walking technique, you should at least try to bend your elbows 90 to 100 degrees when you walk, and concentrate on taking shorter, faster steps. You'll be amazed at how much faster and easier you'll be able to walk.

Joy Grodnick on:
Using Racewalking Technique for a Faster Marathon

Age: 43
Marathon PR: 5:02:29
Marathons Completed: Chicago '99, Rock & Roll '00, First Light '01.

Joy Grodnick was one of my 1999 Chicago Marathon "Team in Training" marathoners. She was a little faster than the rest of our group so I walked with Joy during the race while my co-coach took care of the rest of the team. We had experimented with racewalking technique during our long walks, but Joy said she didn't want to racewalk the marathon. So I had to trick her into it…

Joy says: "My goal for the Chicago Marathon was to finish under 6 hours. My training had gone pretty well so I was pretty sure I could do the time, but I also knew I would not be able to go much faster than that pace. After the first few miles my coach, who was walking with me, suggested I racewalk for a few minutes every mile just to give my walking muscles a break. Whenever I switched over to racewalking technique I would set a goal for myself: I would convince myself to continue racewalking just to the next turn or the next traffic cop. It felt good to give my walking muscles a rest, and the racewalking 'breaks' actually brought my overall mile pace down by about one minute per mile. In fact, the racewalking breaks helped so much that by 20 miles my coach told me that I'd be able to break 5 ½ hours if I kept going at the same pace!

"I have to admit I was a little tired during the last few miles, but I was elated when I saw my time as I crossed the finish line: 5:26:11! I never thought I'd be able to finish that fast. But after my Chicago experience I think I can go even faster. I still don't think I want to racewalk a whole marathon, but I will try to do a little bit more racewalking in training so I can take longer and faster racewalking breaks the next time."

Chapter 8

Marathon Physiology

The human body is an amazing machine; a collection of extremely efficient physiological systems capable of doing amazing things— if properly trained to do them. Our ability to adapt to our environment and to the stresses we impose upon ourselves in training is the reason we're able to change ourselves from sedentary couch potatoes to marathoners. Knowing a bit about these incredible systems will help you to do the kinds of things in training that will help your body to make that incredible transformation.

Solar, gas or batteries?

Our bodies are a lot like hybrid cars that can run on a number of different fuel systems. But instead of using solar panels, batteries, liquid propane and gasoline engines, we create energy through the aerobic (with oxygen) combustion of fats and carbohydrates when walking slowly; by anaerobic (without oxygen) combustion of carbohydrates when walking, racewalking, or running at a faster pace; and through the direct utilization of adenosine triphosphate (ATP) and creatine phosphate (CP) when sprinting.

Under any conditions we only get about five percent of our metabolic energy from protein. The remaining 95% comes from a mix of fats and carbohydrates. The percentage of each fuel we use when we walk is determined by the amount of oxygen that we can supply to the muscles, and the muscles' ability to utilize that oxygen.

Like the hybrid car, our bodies tend to use the most efficient system available under the prevailing operating conditions. Since some "fuels" are more efficient, more plentiful in the body, or more readily utilized than others, our muscles must "decide" which system to "switch on" under different conditions—these conditions being the duration and the pace of the workout or race.

Pros and cons

Each system has its advantages and flaws. Fat is a great fuel source because it's very energy-dense and it exists in the body in abundant quantities. But fat can only be burned in the presence of both oxygen and glycogen (intra-muscular carbohydrate), so it can only be used as a "low-speed" fuel. That's because when you walk at a very fast pace you aren't able to breathe in oxygen at a fast enough rate to break down a high percentage of fat. But that's not a problem when you walk at a slower pace for long distances, so fat is the perfect fuel source for walking a marathon.

Carbohydrates are a more versatile fuel source than fats since they can be burned either with or without oxygen. But since we can only store a limited supply of carbohydrate in our bodies, carbs can be depleted within as little as 90 minutes of hard work—so you won't get very far into your marathon using carbohydrates as your primary fuel source.

Glycolysis, the combustion of carbohydrates for energy, is "bad" for another reason: It's your body's equivalent of a diesel engine—a reliable energy system under a variety of conditions, but when oxygen is limited it's "dirty" as heck. Instead of spewing out smog, however, your anaerobic glycolysis "engine" spits out buckets of nasty lactic acid. The faster you walk, the more lactate you accumulate in your blood and muscles.

Lactic acid is a biochemical "bad guy" because it slows down enzymatic activity within the muscles, preventing them from contracting rapidly. The higher the acid levels, the harder it is for the muscles to contract. Your *lactate threshold* or *anaerobic threshold* is the highest walking intensity at which your body can still produce energy and muscular contractions aerobically, without accumulating fatiguing levels of lactic acid.

It's all about oxygen

Ultimately, the availability of oxygen will dictate how energy is produced in your muscles, and how "clean" the combustion will be. When walking a marathon, most of your energy is produced aerobically, so the bulk of your training for these races should be easy aerobic distance work. Too much speed work will teach your muscles to rely on anaerobic glycolysis, resulting in excess production of lactic acid, and rapid depletion of your carbohydrate stores when racing—not a good scenario.

As walking intensity increases, so does your oxygen intake, or VO_2 (V for Volume, O_2 for oxygen). VO_2 *max* is a measure of the maximum amount of oxygen that your lungs can take in and send to the working muscles. Oxygen has to get to those muscles somehow, and it does so bonded to the hemoglobin in the blood, which is pumped throughout the body by the heart. As oxygen demands increase, heart rate increases—in lock step with respiration rate. Heart rate, then, is a very reliable—albeit indirect—indicator of oxygen use. So heart rate can be used to tell you which systems are producing energy at any given pace.

Your lactate threshold, VO_2 max and your *economy*—the percentage of your VO_2 max that you can maintain during a race without accumulating exhausting amounts of lactic acid—determine, for the most part, how well you can perform in an endurance event like walking a marathon. Luckily, each of these variables, as well as overall endurance, can be improved with training.

The lean, mean walkin' machine

Obviously there's a lot going on "inside" when you train or race. The muscles need to have lots of enzymatically "ready" *mitochondria* and they need to be supplied with lots of oxygen to turn food into energy aerobically. If they don't get enough oxygen the muscles will have to burn a lot of carbohydrates instead of fats, which will lead to carbohydrate depletion in the marathon. So the lungs have to be able to draw in lots of oxygen, the heart has to be able to pump it throughout the body within the blood, and the circulatory system has to have lots of capillaries (tiny blood vessels) to get that oxygen-rich blood into the working muscles. Finally, the neuromuscular system must be highly coordinated so that you can walk with fast, economical (oxygen-sparing) technique. All of these systems have to be working efficiently for you to be truly "race ready." And to get them that way you need to put this book down every once in a while so you can get out the door and walk. Different types of workouts are used to train each of these systems. The next chapter will discuss each of these types of training, and how they can be combined to make you a better marathon walker.

Fat Ain't Just "Dead Weight"

I've heard coaches say that carrying around an extra 10 pounds of body fat is like trying to walk while wearing a 10-pound backpack. Wrong! I'd rather race with a *30 pound* backpack than carry an extra 10 pounds of fat around my midsection—and not because I'm worried about how I look at the beach. You see, fat is not just dead weight; it's a metabolic leach that siphons away valuable oxygen-rich blood that should be going to your muscles. While muscles "pull their own weight" by using that oxygen to create energy to propel you forward, excess fat stores do nothing to move you towards the finish line—despite being perfused with miles of capillaries.

VO2 max, which measures your body's ability to take in and use oxygen to create energy, is measured in milliliters of oxygen per kilogram of body mass per minute. Unless you've studied Einstein's *General Theory of Relativity* before lacing up your walking shoes, and you plan on walking near the speed of light, a minute is always going to be 60 seconds. The other two variables—the amount of oxygen you're able to breathe in and your body mass—are subject to change. So to increase your VO2 max—and greatly improve your race times—you either have to improve your ability to take in oxygen by doing very difficult VO2 max interval workouts, or you can decrease your body mass by simply losing a few extra pounds.

What would you rather do: Go to the track to do lung-searing 800-meter repeats at 98% of maximum heart rate, or simply walk a few extra easy miles per day and decrease your weekly donut intake? It's your decision, Gordita, but I'm putting down the bear claws and going for a walk...

Chapter 9

Types of Workouts

Improvements in fitness come from stressing the body, then allowing it to recover from the stress. Known as the General Adaptation Syndrome, or GAS, this principle is the foundation upon which all endurance training is built. You need to walk long or fast a few days per week to stress the body, then take it easy to allow your body to recover fully, adapt, and rebuild itself stronger than it was before the stress of the hard training.

It's a pretty neat process: Even if you're a knucklehead like me, your body is actually pretty smart—and it doesn't like to feel cruddy. So if you work hard enough to beat up your muscles and make yourself feel like garbage, your body tries to find a way to avoid feeling that way the next time. With enough rest, good diet, clean living and happy thoughts it builds itself up again a little bit stronger than it was before the hard workout, "guessing" that you'll probably go out and do the same crazy thing all over again next week. Your job is to continue upping the ante by increasing the mileage or intensity (speed) of your workouts so that there's always a reasonable level of stress to adapt to. If you don't make your training harder over time your body doesn't really have anything to adapt to, so it won't get any stronger. Any marathon training schedule must include sufficient, and sufficiently varied, hard work to stress all the physiological systems that will be called upon when racing. And this hard work must be interspersed with plenty of rest to allow for complete recovery from, and adaptation to, the hard efforts.

There are five different types of workouts that you can incorporate into your marathon training, each undertaken at a specific range of speeds or heart rate values, and each affecting different physiological systems. They are: long slow distance (LSD) workouts, lactate threshold (LT) workouts, long sub-threshold (LST) workouts, economy workouts, and finally, easy recovery workouts to allow your body to recuperate from the other four types. Maximum efficiency in training comes from using these types of workouts and eliminating "junk mileage"—walks at a pace or heart rate that falls outside the target ranges of these workouts.

Beginning marathoners who are just trying to get through their first marathon safely will do mostly long slow distance workouts and recovery workouts, with an occasional economy workout thrown in for technique development. More advanced walkers will add lactate threshold and long sub-threshold workouts so they can not only get through their marathons, but get through them *faster*.

Rest/recovery workouts

What a great way to start things off! Recovery workouts can be either very easy walking, easy cross-training, or total rest. Since gains in fitness only occur after recovery from and adaptation to hard work, these can be viewed as some of the most important workouts of the week. But they can also be the most difficult to do properly. Sometimes you'll feel pretty good the day after a hard day. So good that you don't want to take an easy day or a day off, even if you need to. But do it. Rest, or enjoy those easy miles now or you'll pay later with injuries, fatigue, or a compromised immune system brought on by overtraining.

Don't get caught up in compulsively tracking weekly mileage. If you need to take a day off, don't worry about bringing down your weekly mileage total. Your ultimate goal shouldn't be to see how many miles you can rack up each week. Your goal should be improvement as a marathon walker, and that's not going to happen if your body can't recover from the hard workouts. You do get some endurance benefits from the miles you walk on your easy days, but doing too much work on these easy days may prevent you from achieving the kind of quality you need on your hard days.

To allow full recovery, you need to walk at a very comfortable pace—going faster on your easy days won't really give you any additional endurance benefits, and your body won't be able to fully recover from your hard workouts. And don't be afraid to cross-train. Swim, roller blade, or go for a long hike. Do something *fun!* If you're too tired to do any kind of workout, get some Ben and Jerry's, flick on the tube and put your feet up. That way you'll be rested *and* you'll be motivated to walk extra long or hard the next day to burn off those 30 grams of milk fat you've sent coursing through your arteries.

Distance training

Distance work is the "heart" of any marathon training program. These workouts improve cardiac efficiency; increase capillary supply to the muscles; increase the size and number of mitochondria in the muscle cells and stimulate their activity in metabolizing both fats and carbohydrates. Distance workouts also help you to develop coordination and efficient walking technique; strengthen ligaments and tendons; build mental "toughness" and basically teach your body to keep going at a reasonable pace for very long distances—and that's exactly what marathons are all about.

Maintaining a relatively high weekly mileage level, and/or doing a weekly long walk at 70 to 75% of maximum heart rate for anywhere from 90 minutes to five hours are the best ways to develop endurance. The long walk should make up about 25 to 30% of your weekly mileage, with shorter walks during the week adding to your overall weekly mileage. Your long walks shouldn't be killer workouts: They should be long slow distance (LSD) workouts done at a comfortable, "conversational" pace. Doing them faster doesn't really give you any additional endurance benefits, and they can break your body down if you do them too fast too often.

Early in your marathon training your longest walks may "only" be about six or eight miles. But towards the end of a 16- or 20-week training program you'll build up to an 18- to 20-mile walk every two weeks. Increasing the distance of your long walks is easy. All you have to do is add one mile to the distance of your longest walk every week. Once you reach 10 miles you'll add two miles to your long day every other week until you get up to 20 miles at a nice easy pace. The alternate week you'll "only" walk 10 or 12 miles, but you'll walk these workouts at a somewhat faster pace.

Right now 20 miles may seem like a pretty tall order, but my Team in Training walkers always tell me that after 16 weeks of training, their last 20-miler before the actual marathon is easier to get through than our first 8-mile group workout. And if you make it through one or two 20-mile walks in training, I guarantee you the marathon will be a piece of cake. One way to make the distance seem more palatable is to think in terms of time walked rather than distance covered. On my beginners' schedule the long walks are between two and five hours. If you can't quite cover the whole 20 miles in 5 hours, don't sweat it. The important thing is the time on your feet, not the distance covered.

Lactate threshold training

If you're training for your first marathon your only goal should be to finish. But if you've walked a marathon before, the next time you'll probably want to walk a little faster. And if you want to race a fast marathon, from time to time you're going to have to train fast. Lactate threshold training is fast training at roughly the same pace that you would walk a hard 10K race. These are walks at a pace or heart rate that's very close to your "lactate threshold"—the speed or heart rate that causes lactic acid to be produced in your muscles at the same rate that your body can break it down. This threshold point can be determined in an exercise physiology laboratory either by drawing blood for lactate analysis while you walk or run on a treadmill, or by graphing your heart rate against your walking speed and "eyeballing" the deflection point or "turn point" where the increase in your heart rate with increasing walking speed begins to level off. But there are several much easier ways to determine the proper pace to walk these workouts:

- **The talk test:** Lactate threshold occurs at the point where you can say at most three or four words before having to gasp for air. If you're able to discuss dialectic materialism you're probably going a little too slowly.

- **The Borg test:** Any time I've had my lactate threshold tested in a physiology lab I've been hooked up to a respiratory gas analyzer and an EKG, and had men in white coats drawing my blood every few minutes to test it in a lactate analyzer. But while all these million-dollar machines were doing their work, the techies would ask me every few minutes to point to a beat up piece of poster board that was taped to the wall. On it were written the numbers 6 through 20, which corresponded to increasing levels of exertion. Each number on the scale—named the "Borg Scale" after the Swedish scientist who created it—had its own descriptive term varying from "very, very easy" for number 6, to something like "blood coming out of your ears hard" for 20. And when the EKG, and the blood lactate analyzer, and the respiratory gas chromatograph all indicated I was at

51

lactate threshold, I, like most athletes, pointed to number 17—which was described on the scale as "moderate discomfort." And that's just the way you should feel when you're at threshold. The pace shouldn't be particularly easy, but not horribly painful either.

- **The one-hour test:** Threshold equates very closely to the pace a well-trained walker can race for fifty minutes to one hour before exhaustion. If you're an experienced racewalker, that corresponds pretty closely to your pace for an eight- to ten-kilometer race.

Threshold workouts should be used sparingly during marathon training—in most cases no more than about once every week or two. And they should only be attempted after you've been doing marathon base training for at least two to three months, and only after you've done a complete warm-up. There are two different types of threshold workouts: lactate threshold intervals and "tempo walks."

Threshold intervals. Intervals, or "speed workouts" are bouts of hard work interspersed with short rest periods. The rest intervals allow you to walk faster during the hard bouts, and will also allow you to do more total work without tiring. In general, the recovery between each repeat is brief—long enough to ensure that you can maintain solid technique, but not so long that your heart rate drops precipitously. Examples of interval workouts are repeat kilometers ("Ks"), repeat miles, and repeat 2Ks or 3Ks with anywhere from one to three minutes of rest between each. (One kilometer is .62 miles, or 2½ laps on a standard high school track. One mile is about 4 laps, 2K is 5 laps and 3K is 7½ laps).

Repeats can also be done as ascending, descending, or up and down "ladders" or "pyramids." An example of a pyramid is a workout of 400 meters, 800 meters, 1,600 meters, 800 meters, 400 meters, all at about 10K race pace, with easy 200-meter recoveries between each hard interval. (200 meters is half a lap on a standard high school track, 400 meters is one lap, 800 meters is two laps, and 1,600 meters—just short of one mile—is four laps.) The pace for these repeats should be faster than your marathon goal pace but no faster than your 10K race pace.

Tempo walks. Occasionally going a little faster during your distance workouts, especially closer to your marathon, is a great way to get yourself really "race ready." But this type of training can be very stressful since your heart rate will be sustained at about 80 to 85% of maximum for two to six miles of walking.

These are so-called "steady-state" tempo workouts because you maintain a steady effort throughout the walk. Another variation is an "acceleration tempo" workout. You start an acceleration tempo workout at about the same pace that you would walk on your long easy days, but then you gradually increase the pace throughout the workout, finishing the last few kilometers as fast as your half-marathon race pace. This has the effect of taking you through all the stages you would go through during a long race, from a very relaxed comfortable state in the early miles to a much more stressful all-out effort in the closing miles. Walking a five- to ten-kilometer race every two or three weeks is a fun way to do your marathon tempo walks.

You should finish any threshold interval workout or tempo session feeling tired, but with enough energy left so you could theoretically take a short break and then repeat the workout. The gains in speed can be considerable if lactate threshold intervals or tempo workouts are used properly, but there is always the danger of pushing too hard and killing yourself for the rest of the week's training. Too much speed work can also convert your fabulous marathon-ready aerobic muscle fibers to anaerobic ones. That's exactly what you want if you're trying to become a world-class sprinter, but those anaerobic muscle fibers will become very fatigued in all but the shortest races if you've done too much speed work. That's because those "fast-twitch" anaerobic muscle fibers burn up lots of carbohydrates instead of fats, and also create lactic acid as a by-product of energy production.

To beat the car metaphor to death, it's a lot like driving your car on the highway too fast. You'll be able to go 26.2 miles on a gallon of gasoline if you drive at a reasonable speed, but you may only be able to go 16 or 18 miles before "running out of gas" if you drive way over the speed limit. So to get yourself to the finish line without running out of gas, train for endurance first, then use speed workouts only occasionally to top off your speed and fitness in the weeks leading up to your marathon.

Long sub-threshold work

Long sub-threshold (LST) workouts are a variation on tempo walks. The only difference is that they are longer, and a little bit slower. These are often called "marathon pace workouts." The idea is to walk at or near your expected marathon pace for a significant percentage of the marathon duration—generally from 40 to 75% of the marathon distance (10 to 20 miles).

Long sub-threshold workouts are used to train the same physiological systems that you will be using during the marathon, but without subjecting yourself to the kind of muscle soreness that the last six to ten miles of the race can bring. They are also very good for testing whether your marathon goal pace is realistic.

LST walks are very tough workouts. First-time marathon walkers should probably skip long sub-threshold workouts altogether, and even more advanced walkers should use them sparingly. But they are the most reliable tool in the box if you want to walk a really fast marathon. If you've already done a marathon and are quite comfortable with long easy walks, you can make the transition into walking LST workout by gradually increasing the pace of your ten- to fifteen-mile efforts.

I'll usually do one long easy walk of eighteen to twenty miles on Sundays, then a long sub-threshold walk of about fifteen miles on Thursdays. Most people don't have time for a long sub-threshold workout during the week, so I recommend walking long and easy one weekend, and then not so long but harder on the alternate weekend. Sometimes I may even combine my long slow distance and long sub-threshold workouts on the same day by starting my 18- to 20-mile workouts at a very comfortable pace and then accelerating to marathon goal pace or faster during the second half of the workout. I think accelerating through your long walks makes a great workout even better because it gives you the best of both worlds, but do whatever works for you. Any way you can get the LST workouts in, they're guaranteed to help you to a faster marathon.

Economy training

There's only one way to learn to walk fast, and that's by walking fast. Economy repeats *will* get you to walk fast! These sessions, also known as efficiency workouts or rhythm workouts, consist of very fast, but very short repeats that force your technique and physiological systems beyond the point at which they are now operating efficiently. They teach your neuromuscular system to fire very rapidly, maximizing stride rate so you'll feel comfortable at more reasonable speeds—including your race speed. Economy repeats are the fastest walking you'll ever do, even faster than your 5K race pace, albeit for much shorter distances.

Marathon walkers don't have to go all out during their economy workouts. For a sprinter these workouts are used to develop raw, explosive speed, but all you're really trying to do as a marathoner is get some life back into your legs after your longer, slower workouts. The pace should be fairly fast, but only about one and a half minutes per mile faster than your marathon goal pace. For example, if you plan on walking your marathon at a pace of 12 minutes per mile, you should do 200-meter to 400-meter repeats at about 10:30 pace (1:18 for each 200-meter interval or 2:37 for each 400-meter interval).

I usually do a long warm-up, then twelve to sixteen 200-meter intervals, or six to eight 400-meter intervals at least once per week to perk my legs up after my long day. I'll also do a few short (50- to 100-meter) economy intervals as part of my warm-up before any race or threshold workout, and may even throw in a few surges (fast bursts) during a long walk to make sure my technique is quick and efficient.

If you learn to walk efficiently at very high speed, your marathon race pace will be faster as well, without making any other changes to your training. In fact, economy work will help you to walk with less effort at any pace or distance. I recommend that any marathon walker do frequent economy work to develop and maintain quick and efficient walking technique. But it's important to start slowly and build gradually. The bursts are short during an economy workout, but any time you walk very fast you run the risk of straining your muscles. So be sure to start the workout with a complete warm-up, then do only three or four intervals the first time and work up from there. If you feel any muscle pain at all, back off the pace immediately.

Heart rate monitors

A lot of walkers use heart rate monitors to gauge whether they are training too hard, or not hard enough. But what are they, and how do they work?

Once again, the story begins with oxygen, which has to get to the working muscles somehow. The oxygen travels from your lungs to the muscles by bonding to hemoglobin in your blood. The oxygen-rich blood is then pumped throughout the body by the heart. As oxygen needs increase, heart rate increases—in lock-step with respiration rate. So heart rate is a very reliable, albeit indirect, indicator of oxygen use. That's why the Neanderthals (back in the 1960s and '70s) used to stop to take their pulse during workouts. But who wants to stop in the middle of a workout to poke around looking for an artery? By the time you find the thing, then count to six or ten, your pulse has dropped 20 beats anyway, rendering the results meaningless. But there's a better way...

With each beat, the heart generates electrical signals that can be measured on the surface of the skin. A heart rate monitor transmitter contains two electrodes to detect these signals. The electrodes are mounted within the sealed transmitter that's attached to the chest with an elastic belt. The transmitter detects the voltage differential on the skin during every heartbeat and relays the signal to a wrist receiver, which displays heart rate in beats per minute.

Dr. Seppo "Say it Three Times Fast" Säynäjäkangas produced the first portable heart rate monitors in Finland in 1982, and by 1990 Polar was distributing a full line of inexpensive models to the U.S. and world markets. Today, several manufacturers produce monitors for under $100, which makes them accessible to even the most recreational athletes.

If you know your maximum heart rate (the maximum number of times your heart can beat in one minute) you can use a heart rate monitor to tell you how hard you should be walking for any kind of workout. But how do you determine your maximum heart rate?

The most accurate way is to do something that actually gets your heart working up to maximum while wearing a heart rate monitor—but you have to be very well rested, and be willing to push yourself extremely hard to do that. The safest way to push yourself hard enough to find your *true* maximum heart rate is to get yourself up to maximum during a cardiologist's treadmill stress test—assuming the doctor allows you to push yourself all out. But with malpractice lawyers multiplying like rabbits, doctors rarely do push you to 100% during a stress test, so let the doc know ahead of time that you actually do want to get yourself up to max.

You can also get yourself up to maximum by running or racewalking a series of three or four very hard 400-meter intervals at near 100% effort. Take one-minute rest between each, then really blast the end of your last one. Your heart rate should definitely be at maximum—assuming your technique is good enough to get you up to maximum. Fitness walking technique isn't efficient enough to allow you to push yourself to maximum, so you'll have to run or racewalk the intervals instead of walking them.

A good "cheat" is to wear a heart rate monitor during a hard 5-kilometer race. If you're really pushing during the race, your heart rate should get up to about 90% of maximum. So you can estimate your maximum heart rate by dividing your 5K-race heart rate by .90. For example, if you sustain a heart rate of 180 beats per minute towards the end of a 5K race, your maximum heart rate is about 180/.90 or 200 beats per minute (BPM).

The *easiest* way to get an *estimate* of your maximum heart rate is to use simple formula. For men, subtracting your age from 220 gives you an estimate of your maximum heart rate. So if you are a 40-year-old male, your maximum heart rate should be about 220-40 or 180. For women the formula is 226-age. There are a number of variations on these formulas, but unfortunately every one of them can be wildly inaccurate, especially for fitter people and older people. Any of the other methods I've mentioned previously will give a better estimate because they are based on what *your* heart does rather than what the average person's heart does.

Once you know your maximum heart rate you can determine heart rate levels for any kind of workout. For a recovery day you should only work at 60 to 70% of maximum, or a range of 120 to 140 beats per minute if your maximum heart rate is 200 BPM. On your long easy days you can allow your heart rate to climb up to 75% of maximum; long sub-threshold workouts should get you up to about 80% of maximum; and tempo walks should get you to 85%. For marathon training you should never allow your heart rate to get over 90% of maximum, even during interval workouts.

How to Use a Heart Rate Monitor

There are a number of different ways a heart rate monitor can be used in training and racing:

As an Equalizer. External factors such as heat, humidity, altitude and wind, and internal factors like dehydration, fatigue and psychological stress can profoundly affect your ability to perform. Ignoring these factors by attempting to train or race at a set pace per mile under difficult conditions can lead to overtraining or "hitting the wall" (Chapter 25) in your marathon. A heart rate monitor allows you to train or race at an even effort under any conditions.

As a Governor. Sometimes it's hard to go easy. A monitor can ensure that LSD really is long *slow* distance and recovery days truly are recovery days. It can also ensure that you don't go too crazy in the first few miles of a marathon. There's no such thing as "free" energy: If you go out too hard at the start, you'll pay for it at the end.

As a Butt-Kicker. Sorry, but there are also days when you have to work pretty hard to get fitter. A heart rate monitor can ensure that you're sustaining an 80% effort during long sub-threshold workouts, an 85% effort during tempo workouts and 90% during threshold intervals.

As a Diagnostician. Keeping track of morning heart rate can give you forewarning that you're over-training. If your resting heart rate is five to eight beats per minute higher than normal, it's time to back off: You're overtrained, and possibly on the verge of getting sick or injured.

Whether you're training for your first marathon, or your 51st, you can benefit from a heart rate monitor's ability to keep you motivated, under control, and "in the zone."

Caveats

Never completely trash yourself in any of your workouts—long-term gains don't come from single super-human efforts, but from consistent long-term training. A single workout will not affect overall conditioning much, but if the intensity is too high you can push yourself over the edge and become "overtrained," or worse yet, injured. Save it for the race! Also:

- **Warm-up completely!** Always, always, always do a complete warm-up before any fast workout. Walk at an easy pace for ten or fifteen minutes, then do some easy flexibility drills (Chapter 11) and stretches (Chapter 12) followed by a few gradual accelerations. Then and only then should you begin the workout. If you're unsure of your pace, start out conservatively, then build up to faster walking through the course of the workout.

- **Stay hydrated!** Muscles are about 75% water, so even slightly dehydrated muscles are inefficient, injury-prone muscles. Keep a water bottle with you at all times, both while training, and around the home or office. It's cheap, readily-available, has no calories, and doesn't stain, smell or rot your teeth, so drink up! And while you're at it…

- **Carb up!** Marathon training burns a lot of calories. That's the good news *and* the bad news. Those long walks can deplete your muscles of glycogen (carbohydrates) which is one of the primary causes of overtraining. Drink some sort of carbohydrate-rich sports drink starting after the first eight miles or so of your long walks, and continue after you finish the workout. Then be sure to eat a hearty carbohydrate and protein-rich meal within the first few hours of finishing your walk when your muscles are most receptive to absorbing carbohydrates.

- **Listen to your body!** Don't be a slave to your training schedule. There will be some days when you're just too tired to do the workout you have scheduled. It's okay! Take those rest and recovery days when your body says you need them, not when the calendar says you should. It's always better to be slightly undertrained than overtrained.

- **Stretch!** Long-distance walking causes your major muscle groups to tighten, and tight muscles are much more likely to cramp or tear than flexible muscles. Stretching, especially gentle stretching after training, will help to keep those walking muscles loose and healthy.

Chapter 10

Cross-training

Cross-training certainly can't take the place of your walking workouts, but occasionally using other activities for *supplemental* conditioning can be beneficial. You don't become a great pianist by practicing on a kazoo, and you aren't going to walk a fast marathon by swimming a mile a day without any walking. But if you've done your walk training, cross-training can be used to build general endurance while giving the walking muscles a break. It can also be a great tool for continuing to train through a walking injury.

Specificity

Hard as it may be to imagine, there may be days when you just don't want to walk, but you *do* want to give some of your walking muscles a good workout. Some cross-training activities use a lot of the same muscle groups you use when walking. Certainly hiking would be the most similar to your walk training because it's basically just walking in a different setting—in the woods instead of on the roads. But there are other activities that give your major walking muscles a good workout. Roller bladeing, cross-country skiing and using machines like elliptical trainers, stair steppers and NordicTraks are great walking substitutes because they use a lot of the same muscles.

Whichever activity you choose, try to make sure your cross-training is as walking-specific as possible. Take short, quick steps on the stair stepper or NordicTrak rather than long slow strides. Use short strokes instead of long sweeping ones and bend your elbows and pump your arms vigorously when roller bladeing, and take short, shuffling strides without lifting your knees too high when running.

Variety

Other times, your goal when cross-training will be to build endurance and to reinforce a quick turnover rate while giving your muscles and your mind a break from the miles and miles of walking you do as a marathoner-in-training. Your goal should not be to see how good a biker, runner or pogo-stick jumper you can become. So take it easy, and choose cross-training activities that you enjoy. If you like to run, run. If you like to roller blade, roller blade. If you like to bike, grease up your chain and go. But don't overdo any one activity. Instead, use a variety of activities to keep things interesting, and to work more and different muscle groups.

Recovery

The main advantage of cross-training is that it gives you a good cardio-vascular workout while giving your tired walking muscles a break. So take it easy. You're supposed to be recovering from your walking workouts, so don't go nuts. Even though you might be strong enough to walk for two hours, that doesn't mean you'll be able to go out for a two-hour bike ride without causing a lot of soreness in your under-used biking muscles. Start out with a 15-minute ride, then see how beat-up you are the next day. If you don't feel any undue muscle soreness, build up gradually from there, adding about 15 minutes to your workout with each session.

Injury rehabilitation

Walking is one of the safest fitness pursuits you can find, but no activity is 100% injury-free. If you do get injured, cross-training is a great way to stay fit while you recover. If you can't walk on the roads or treadmill without pain, try walking in the deep end of a swimming pool while wearing a floatation vest. You use all the same muscles that you do while training on dry land, but with zero impact. Most health clubs have some sort of flotation devices that will keep your head above water. NordicTraks or elliptical trainers are also good low-impact substitutes when you aren't able to walk.

What About Weights?

I think of weight training as supplemental training, as opposed to cross-training. There aren't a lot of aerobic benefits in lifting weights, but they are great for injury prevention, and for developing strength and flexibility.

- **Strength.** Your muscles are what propel you forward when you walk. The stronger your legs and arms are relative to your body mass, the faster you will walk. And strong abdominals will help you to keep your posture when you get tired at the end of a marathon or long workout, and will help prevent lower back pain.

- **Flexibility.** Weights are also great for developing lasting flexibility. Lift relatively light weights through a full range of motion rather than trying to lift as much as you can in a few lifts.

- **Injury Prevention.** Strong, flexible muscles will not only help you to walk faster, they will also allow you to do so with much less risk of injury.

Try to work the major muscles of the legs, arms and abdomen. The best thing to do is set up an appointment with a personal trainer or fitness instructor at your local gym. Let him or her know that you are planning to walk a marathon. If there's time, walk on a treadmill for the trainer so he or she can point out any areas of weakness that you should be working on.

Prioritization

To walk a marathon, you'll have to walk a lot of miles in training. So obviously, making sure you get those walking workouts in should always be your first priority. But if you have the time, what other activities should you do to help your walking? If I have some extra time after my walks, my priorities are as follows:

- **Stretching.** Stretching is one of the most important things you can do to stay injury-free. No matter how busy you are you should always make time to stretch, *especially* after your workouts.

- **Abdominal work.** Crunches and sit-ups (Chapter 12) are great for strengthening the muscles that help you to maintain your posture when you're tired, and help you to achieve quick, powerful strides. Strong abdominals can also help to reduce lower back pain.

- **Cross-training.** If you still have time in your training week after your walking, stretching, and abdominal work, you may want to add some cross-training which will contribute to cardiovascular fitness and strength without fatiguing your walking muscles.

- **Weight-lifting.** I think muscular strength is important for walkers, both for speed and injury-prevention, but unless I'm rehabilitating an injury, weights fall last on my list of training priorities. If I *am* recovering from an injury, rehabilitating the problem area with weights becomes one of my top priorities.

Final thoughts

Some of the top marathon walkers in the world spend hours per week lifting weights, stretching, doing drills, and cross-training. Others spend very little time on these activities. But ALL good walkers walk a lot. With limited hours in the day to train, your walking workouts are by far the most important workouts you can do to help your walking. But supplemental activities can be an effective way to build strength and to improve cardio-vascular conditioning, flexibility, and reduce the likelihood of injuries. So make sure you get out there and walk (and stretch afterwards!), and if there's a little free time in your schedule, don't be afraid to mix in some cross-training, weights and abdominal work on your easy days.

Chapter 11

Dynamic Flexibility Drills

Athough the stretching exercises introduced in the next chapter are very important in increasing *static* flexibility, they're only part of the story. Static stretches do help develop long-term gains in flexibility, which will help prevent injuries, but they give better results when used *after* training. Since walking is a *dynamic* activity, static stretches are of limited value in preparing the body to walk.

Marathon walkers should do *dynamic flexibility drills* before each workout to increase their flexibility throughout the dynamic range of the walking motion. Dynamic flexibility drills can also be used as technique drills to help develop walking-specific neuromuscular coordination.

Specific drills

The following drills should be used as part of your daily warm-up routine—especially on speed work and competition days. Always start slowly, and always precede your flexibility drills with at least a half mile of easy walking to get the blood flowing. Work up from a few repetitions at first to 12 to 15 repetitions of each exercise, and gradually increase the range of motion from one repetition to the next until full extension is reached over the last few repeats. Always maintain good posture when doing drills, and don't overdo it—work the muscles through a sufficient range of motion to allow a good stretch, but not to the point of pain.

1. Leg swings. Stand sideways next to a wall, tree or car, steadying yourself by holding on with one hand. Swing your outside leg from front to back, bending the knee as it comes forward, straightening as it goes back. Accentuate the back portion of the swing to stretch the hamstring, gluteus and lower back muscles. Do 8 to 12 swings, then turn around and repeat with the other leg. Swinging the free arm in the opposite direction of the leg will help develop coordination.

2. Side swings. Stand about two feet from the wall with your feet about shoulder-width apart. Holding on to the wall with both hands, swing your right leg to the outside, then to the inside about 8 to 12 times to stretch the groin and outside of the hip. Repeat with the left leg about 8 to 12 times.

3. Swedish twists. Grab the wall again, standing about 2 feet away. Tuck your right foot behind your left knee, then swing the right knee towards the wall, then back, keeping the foot tucked behind the knee. Repeat 8 to 12 times, then repeat with the other leg. Great for loosening up the lower back and groin.

66

4. Hip circles. Holding on to the wall with both hands, keep your feet about shoulder-width apart. With arms outstretched, lean into the wall with your pelvis, then circumscribe a large circle with your hips to stretch the entire pelvic area. Do 8 to 10 circles clockwise, then 8 to 10 circles counterclockwise.

5. Knee pumps. Hold onto the wall, with feet together about four feet from the wall. Stand on the balls of your feet without bending at the waist. Pump each knee forward quickly, rolling up onto the toes of the pumping foot. Pump each leg 8 to 12 times.

6. Arm swings. With your palms facing outward and elbows straight, "backstroke" with each arm. Do 8 to 12 with each arm for upper body flexibility. Swinging both arms at the same time, 180 degrees apart, is good for developing coordination.

7. Torso twists. Stand with your feet shoulder-width apart, arms outstretched and parallel to the ground. Keeping the feet planted, twist the torso fully by swinging the arms to the left, then to the right. Repeat 8 to 12 times. Great for the lower back and shoulders.

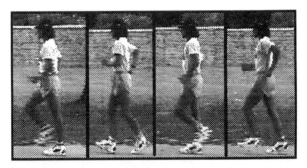

8. Quick steps. Self-explanatory. Walk with an extremely short stride, one heel landing almost on top of the toes of the other foot. Take very quick steps. Reinforces quick turnover and a short stride in front of the body.

After your warm-up and drills, do a few "accelerations" before the start of the workout or race. Start out by walking at an easy pace, then accelerate smoothly to 90% of top speed. Hold that speed for about five to ten seconds, then decelerate. Spending 5 or 10 minutes doing dynamic flexibility drills and accelerations before each workout will give you better range of motion for your workout, and will help you to develop lasting walking-specific coordination.

Chapter 12

Stretching

Walking is a pretty basic activity, but it requires a full range of motion for optimal performance. Unfortunately, marathon walking is an endurance event which, just like marathon running, creates inflexibility in the muscle groups used. When you walk, you're being propelled forward by *contracting* muscles. Over time, these muscles incrementally lose flexibility if they're not stretched gently after each workout. If properly stretched, muscles are lengthened and circulation is enhanced. Increased flexibility enables a more fluid, efficient style that will allow you to walk much faster with reduced chance of injury.

Types of stretches

There are three different types of stretching: ballistic or "bouncy" stretches, static stretches and proprioceptive neuromuscular facilitation (PNF) or "contract/release" stretches.

- **Ballistic stretches.** Ballistic stretches are the old-fashioned military toe touches and the like. They can trigger a protective contraction in the muscle that defeats the purpose of stretching, which is to *loosen* the muscles. Don't use ballistic stretches.

- **Static stretches.** Static stretches are slow easy stretches that are held for at least 20 to 30 seconds. While stretching, breathe normally into the stretch—don't hold your breath. Mild tension should be felt in the muscle, not pain.

- **PNF stretches.** The third type of stretches, PNF exercises, are a way of tricking the neuromuscular system into allowing a deeper stretch than you would otherwise be able to achieve with ordinary static stretches. First the muscle to be stretched is contracted for 10 to 20 seconds, then allowed to relax for three to ten seconds. Then you perform a static stretch for the usual 20 to 30 seconds. The process is repeated several times. Again, don't stretch to the point of pain or else muscle contraction and possible injury may result.

Tight spots

Stretching is most effectively used to improve flexibility in an individual walker's own particular "tight spots." Each walker will have different problem areas, but a few notoriously tight muscle groups common to many walkers are:

1. Hamstrings. The hamstrings are the long muscles at the back of the thigh. Tight, weak hamstrings can limit stride length and they are also one of the most common chronic injury areas for walkers.

To stretch the hamstrings, lie on your back, then raise one leg and grab it with both hands behind the knee. Keep the opposite leg bent and the abdominals tensed to maintain a "pelvic tilt." Tense the ➡ hamstrings for five seconds by pushing against your hands, relax, then pull the leg towards your body to stretch it. Hold for 20 seconds, then repeat with the other leg.

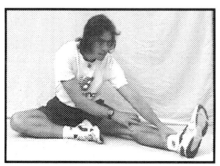

The seated toe-touch is another great hamstring stretch. Sit with one leg bent in front of you, the other leg straight and ⬅ out to the side. With your back flat, reach for the toes on the foot of the straight leg. Hold for 20 to 30 seconds. If you can't reach the foot, use a towel to assist.

Finally, try the "passive hang" to stretch the upper part of the hamstrings and the lower back. Stand with your feet about shoulder-width apart, then simply bend over at the waist and reach for your toes. Hold ➡ the position for about 20 seconds, then repeat with the right leg crossed in front of the left, then again with the left leg crossed in front of the right.

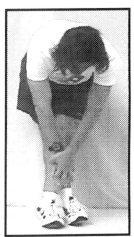

2. Groin/gracilis muscle. The gracilis originates in the groin area and inserts below the knee on the inside of the leg. It's another

commonly injured muscle/tendon complex. To stretch the gracilis, sit on the floor with the soles of your feet together. Press your elbows into your ⬅ inner thighs to provide resistance, then contract for five seconds, attempting to bring the knees together against the resistance. Relax, then stretch by pushing your knees toward the floor for 20 seconds.

The wall straddle is another great gracilis stretch. First sit sideways against a wall, then turn yourself around 90 degrees so you're lying flat on your back with your legs straddling the wall. Let your legs drop until you feel a ➡ good stretch in the groin and along the inside of the thigh. As the muscles relax allow your feet to drop further down the wall. Hold for 30 seconds to several minutes.

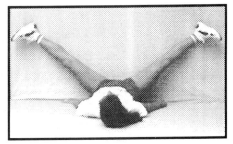

The squat is a great all-around stretch, mainly for the groin, but also for the lower back and calves and Achilles tendon. Simply squat straight

down with your feet flat on the floor, arms hanging in front or holding your ankles for balance.

Finally, try a kneeling squat to really get the inner thigh muscles. Kneel down, extending one leg straight out to the side. ↓

Squat down, pressing the heel into the floor until you feel a good stretch all along the inside of the thigh. Hold for 20 seconds, then do the other side.

3. Quadriceps. The quads are the large muscles at the front of the thighs. Increased quadriceps flexibility will further enhance effective stride length and will facilitate knee straightening if you racewalk.

To stretch the quads, lay on your right side, then grab the left ankle with your left hand and pull back. Pull the leg back and away from the other leg, rather than trying to bring your heel toward your butt, which can strain the ↓ knee. Repeat on the other side.

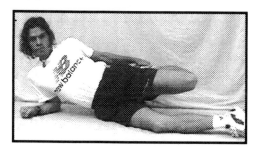

The quad stretch can also be performed while standing, but be sure to hold onto a ➡ wall or other stable support with your free hand.

4. Piriformis/iliotibial band. The piriformis and the iliotibial (I.T.) band both originate in the hip. The piriformis inserts in the upper part of the leg, and the iliotibial band inserts on the outside of the knee. They are both very commonly injured areas in walkers. A tight I.T. band will cause pain in the knee or hip, while a tight piriformis can pinch the sciatic nerve, causing pain to shoot down the leg.

To stretch the iliotibial band, sit with your left leg straight out in front of you, and the right leg bent at the knee with the right foot flat on the floor to the left of the left knee. "Hug" your ➡ right knee, and sitting up straight with good posture, pull the knee towards your chest until you feel a good stretch in the right buttock. To get a deeper

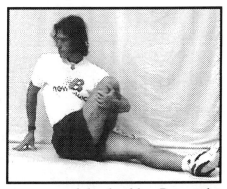

stretch, twist your torso by looking over your right shoulder. Repeat the stretch with the other leg.

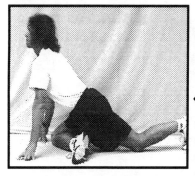

To stretch the piriformis and the I.T. band, start out kneeling with both hands on the floor in front of you. Bring the right knee forward and out to the side so the right foot lies flat under your body, then extend the left leg back behind you so your weight is over the right foot. You should feel a stretch on the outside of the gluteus and along the I.T. band. Hold for 20 seconds then repeat on the other side.

Here's another good stretch for the piriformis: Simply lay flat on your stomach with your knees bent at 90-degree angles. Allow your feet to drop outward, towards the floor until you feel a good stretch on the

outside of the hip, and ➡
in the sacro-iliac joint
of the lower back. It looks
easy, but you'll definitely
feel it!

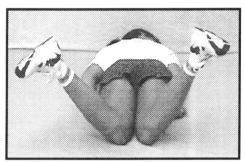

5. Lower back. Nasty lower
back pain has been my
downfall over the years,
causing me to miss more workouts and races than any other injury. Since
tight hamstrings will "pull" at their insertion points in the pelvis,
hamstring stretches will relieve some strain on the lower back. In
addition, try the "brick," the "seal" and the "bow" to specifically stretch
the lower back.

For the brick, you'll need a brick, book,
or piece of wood about one or two inches
thick. Simply stand "at attention" with one
foot on the brick, and the other foot flat on
⬅ the floor, making sure that both knees
remain straight. You should feel a good
stretch right in the sacro-iliac joints of the
lower back, in the gluteus muscles that lead
into them, and at the origin of the iliotibial
band in the hips as well.

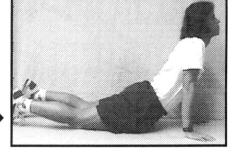

To do the seal, ➡
lay flat on your stomach
with your palms flat on the

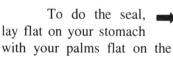

floor. Stretch yourself out, then do a push up. Arch your back while
keeping your belly flat on the floor. Hold for 20 to 30 seconds.

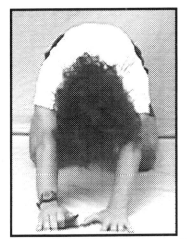

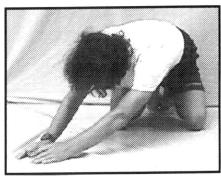

For the bow, kneel down  on all fours with your arms stretched out in front of you and your palms on the floor, then sit back on your heels to stretch the lower back. After 20 seconds, "crawl" with your hands as far as you can to the left, then to the right to stretch out the muscles leading into the sacroiliac joints.

6. Shins. Every time your heel hits the ground when you walk, your foot "dorsi-flexes" or flattens out, which stretches the shin muscles. Unless your shins are well developed from years of walking they may start to hurt during your marathon training. If they do, massage them, then try the following stretch: Sit down "Indian style" with one leg crossed over the other. Dorsi-flex your ankle (bring the top of your foot closer to your shin) while pushing down on the top of the foot with your hand to provide resistance. Hold for five seconds, then relax and stretch, pointing the toes and pulling down with the hand to stretch the shins.

Change the angle of the foot slightly to get both the tibialis anterior muscles on the front of the shin, and the peroneus muscles along the outside of the shin.

7. Hip flexors/iliopsoas. Flexible hip flexors—the muscles at the top front of your thighs, will allow you to achieve an increased stride length behind your body. This provides a longer stride without sacrificing turnover rate, resulting in a more powerful push from the rear.

To stretch the hip flexors, step forward with your left leg so your ➡ left foot is flat on the ground, and your left knee is bent at 90 degrees so your thigh is parallel to the ground. To limit strain on the knee, keep it directly over the foot. Your right leg should be extended way back behind you. Now drop straight down to stretch the iliopsoas—the strongest hip flexor.

8. Calves. More supple calf muscles and increased range of motion in the ankle joint will allow greater rear-stride length and will enable a more powerful toe-off.

Stretch the soleus and ⬅ gastroc nemius muscles of the calf by first standing on your toes for about 10 seconds to ➡ contract the muscles. Relax, then step way back with one foot to stretch the gastroc nemius muscle in the upper part of the calf. Hold for about 20 seconds. To get the soleus muscle in the lower part of the calf, bend the back knee for 20 seconds, keeping the foot flat on the ground.

9. Neck and shoulders. Upper-body relaxation is one of the most important elements of a smooth, efficient walking technique. Tension in the upper body will be transferred to the hips, reducing effective stride length.

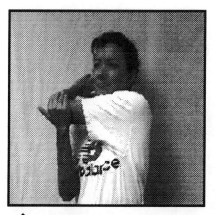

For a great PNF stretch, 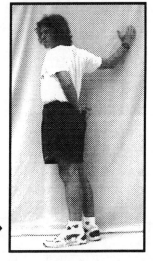 push your head sideways with the palm of your hand for five seconds, then relax. Now pull to the side with the same hand for 15 to 20 seconds to stretch the muscles of the neck, and the trapezius muscle between the neck and shoulder.

↑ To stretch the entire shoulder area, hold your right arm parallel to the ground with the elbow bent at 90 degrees. Push out against your hand for five seconds to contract the sub-scapular muscles, then stretch them by bringing the upper arm toward your chest by pulling from the elbow with your free hand. As always, hold for 20 to 30 seconds.

10. Chest/pectoralis major. Face a wall with your elbow bent at 90 degrees and your forearm vertical—like you're waving to the wall. Push against the wall with the ➡ palm of your hand, your forearm and your biceps for five seconds, then relax. Keeping your arm flat against the wall, turn your body sideways, using the wall to stretch the chest and shoulder muscles. You can also do the same stretch with your arm fully extended to stretch the upper arm and shoulder.

Before or after?

Of course there are many more stretches than the few I've described here, but they are a good starting point. By doing the stretches in the order presented you can begin on the floor, then work up to the standing stretches. You may want to do a few stretches before training to make the workout feel good, but since stretching "cold" muscles can lead to injuries, dynamic flexibility drills are generally better than static stretches for promoting pre-workout flexibility. Long-term gains in flexibility will come from stretching warm muscles *after* your walking workouts.

It's a good idea to spend 5 or 10 minutes gently stretching all the major muscle groups after every workout—especially after the long or fast sessions. You should also try to spend at least one half hour about three times per week on a more comprehensive stretching program for increased range of motion and injury prevention. For more stretches, there are several excellent books available. Bob Anderson's *Stretching* is the best known, but you need to find the particular stretches that work for you, so shop around. Also, experiment to see which positions get it right where it hurts.

Basic stretching principles

- Warm-up or complete your walking workout first to increase circulation before stretching.

- Stretch gently—stop if it hurts.

- Breathe rhythmically.

- Focus on the muscles being stretched.

- Stretch the tighter side first.

- After stretching one group of muscles, stretch the antagonist group—i.e., stretch the quadriceps, then the hamstrings.

- For PNF stretches, tense the muscles to be stretched for 5 to 10 seconds, relax for three to five seconds then stretch for 20 seconds.

- Maintain good posture at all times.

Abdominal work

Although sit ups and crunches aren't actually stretches, it's a good idea to do at least some abdominal work every day as part of your stretching routine. Most of your propulsion when you walk comes from the muscles of the upper leg, butt and hip region, and strong abdominals are a vital component.

The abdominal muscles provide a stable support for many of the large muscle groups of the lower-body, so strengthening the abs will reduce strain on the lower back, and will enable you to take stronger, faster strides when you walk. Try "curl ups" with a pelvic tilt and "crunches" with your legs crossed at the ankles. To work the oblique muscles on the sides of the abdomen, add a rotation of the torso to each side while doing both of these exercises. Work up to three sets of ten reps of each type. When doing crunches, avoid pulling your chin towards your chest, which can stain the neck.

Curl-ups with a pelvic tilt. Start by lying on the floor with your knees bent. Tighten your abdominal muscles to flatten your lower back against the floor. Hold your hands together and slowly curl up. Hold for five seconds then lower yourself down.

Crunches. Start by laying flat on your back with your hands folded behind the back of your head and your legs raised and crossed at the ankles. Curl up towards your knees. Twist to the side while curling up to work the oblique muscles. Work up to three sets of ten repetitions.

Self massage

While doing your stretching exercises, feel around for "knots" in your muscles. These knots of "necrotic tissue" are actually damaged muscle fibers. These knots have the same effect on your muscles as knots in a piece of rope or string: The muscle gets "bunched up" at the damaged spots and is incrementally shortened. By working out the knots with cross-fiber strokes with your fingers, you can help to lengthen and loosen the muscles. Using a small wooden or plastic massage tool will save your fingers from fatigue, and a Thera-cane—a long, curved heavy-duty plastic stick with round knobs at either end—will help you to reach spots you just can't reach with your fingers.

Putting one foot in front of the other for 20 or 30 minutes at a time is quite easy on the body. But extending those workouts to three, four or five hours—not to mention racing for four to eight hours—can start to take a toll on your muscles and joints. But taking care of your body by stretching after every workout, and perhaps gently massaging out any knots that may arise, will keep your muscles loose which will help you to get to the starting line healthy—and to the finish line faster.

Great Walking Marathons:
Dublin Marathon, Dublin, Ireland

The Dublin Marathon is one of the biggest draws for charity marathon walk teams like the Arthritis Foundation's Joints in Motion, the American Diabetes Association's Team Diabetes, and the Leukemia & Lymphoma Society's Team in Training. So much so that every year more than half the field comes from overseas, including several thousand from the U.S. Many of them are walkers, and for good reason. Walkers are permitted an early start and a very generous 9 ½-hour time limit, the weather is almost always perfect, the course relatively flat, and the field size small enough to avoid crowding at aid stations.

Internationally known as the "Friendly Marathon," every aspect of the race weekend is guided by the hand of the proverbial Irish hospitality. And you would be hard pressed to find a marathon with more enthusiastic crowd support than Dublin.

The course starts and finishes on O'Connell Street, Dublin's most famous thoroughfare, in front of the General Post Office, site of the 1916 Easter Rebellion that marked the beginning of independence from Great Britain. The first few miles wind along the Liffey River, through historic Georgian streets and past 500-year-old Trinity College, then on to St. Stephens Green, University College, and Phoenix Park before returning to the finish line back at the GPO.

While many of the best-known international marathons expend most of their resources catering to the elite, with walkers and slower runners picking over the crumbs that fall from the table, Dublin stands out as one race that really "goes the extra mile" to provide walkers with a world-class marathoning experience.

Chapter 13

"The Complete Workout"

Combining marathon training with the rest of your harried life isn't always easy. With a multitude of distractions pulling at you from all directions, your daily workouts often get sandwiched in between other commitments. You know the feeling: You run into the house, throw on your training clothes and hit the roads with barely enough time to tie your shoes. Then after a quick buzz of the neighborhood you shower and change while scarfing down a slice of leftover pizza before stuffing yourself back into the car to head off to your next appointment. Not exactly the life the fitness magazine cover models are living, now is it?

It may be alright to squeeze in a quick three miles between work and the PTA meeting every once in a while, but doing so on a regular basis can leave you tight and injury prone. To maximize your potential and ward off injuries, every workout should be a Complete Workout consisting of a full warm-up, the workout itself, a cool-down, and plenty of stretching.

The warm-up

It's generally believed that cold, tight muscles are more likely to cramp up or pull than warm ones. You'll also have a more fluid, relaxed stride if your muscles are warmed up.

But what goes into a good warm-up? I recommend a three-step procedure. First, you should walk at a very easy pace for 10 to 15 minutes to get the blood flowing. If you're planning on a fast-paced workout, you should consider accelerating throughout the warm-up, starting at a very easy pace and finishing at close to the pace that you'll be walking during the main part of your workout. Then you should use a series of dynamic flexibility drills like legs swings and knee pumps (Chapter 11), and maybe a few static stretches (Chapter 12) to work out any remaining tight spots. Finally, three or four acceleration sprints of 40 to 50 meters will prime the muscles for the task ahead.

The length and intensity of the workout will determine the length and intensity of the warm-up. Shorter, faster workouts require more vigorous warm-ups; longer, slower workouts don't generally require as much. Although you'll probably find that a complete warm-up will keep you from tightening up towards the end of your long walks as well.

The workout

The workout not only dictates the type of warm-up you'll need, it can also be an extension of the warm-up. Whether doing long easy distance or interval repeats, it's not a bad idea to accelerate through your workouts. Start at a very comfortable pace in the first few miles of your long walks or the first few intervals of your repeat workouts, then gradually pick up the pace as your muscles get warmed up. Not only will you be allowing your body to gradually adjust to the increasing intensity, you'll also be teaching yourself to accelerate through or adjust to the increasing fatigue or discomfort you'll experience through the course of your race. Starting your workouts like a bat out of Hades, then "crashing" is the worst thing you can do. Not only will you feel lousy at the end of the workout, you'll wind up teaching yourself to do the same thing in your races.

The cool-down

Do not pass go and do not collect $200 until you've cooled down after your workout. Obviously a cool-down won't help you to walk faster in your workout or race since you do it after you've already finished, but the cool-down will allow you to recover much faster from the hard effort.

Cooling down is easy. Just walk at about the same pace as the start of your warm-up, but only go for about half the time or distance. Five minutes should do the trick for most workouts. After cooling down, don't forget to stretch and rehydrate to speed muscle recovery, and drink a carbo-rich sports drink to speed glycogen replenishment. You can further enhance glycogen uptake by eating more carbohydrates combined with a little protein as soon as your stomach has settled down enough to allow it. I used to think cooling-down after a workout wasn't as important as warming-up before. But over time I started to notice how much better I'd feel the next day if I treated myself to that five-minute cool-down after my workout instead of immediately cramming myself into my car for the drive home.

Final thoughts

The time you spend walking is only one part of a complete workout. You shouldn't even count the mileage if you didn't do your warm-up first, then your drills and accelerations, and then your cool-down, stretches, and maybe some sit-ups after the walk. Unfortunately, when time is limited, this "supplementary" stuff is the first thing to go. Wrong approach! If your time is limited, you'll be much better off in the long run if you do 5 to 10 minutes of drills, 20 minutes of walking, then 5 to 10 minutes of stretching, rather than walking a longer workout without the drills and stretching.

Don't cut corners—always do "complete" workouts, then if you can find the time, do that abominable abdominal work, lift weights, swim and/or cross-train. Doing so will ensure a long, injury-free marathoning career. Ignoring this ancillary work is a sure-fire way to bad technique, sub-par times and nagging injuries.

Chapter 14

Training Schedules

The basic principles of marathon training are the same for everyone: You build sufficient endurance to get yourself through 26.2 miles of walking by gradually increasing the distance of a weekly or bi-weekly long easy walk. Then closer to the marathon you do a certain amount of training at your marathon pace or faster to get yourself ready to walk that 26.2 miles at a solid pace.

The long easy walks are what get you through the race safely. They build the muscle and joint strength that keep you injury-free, and they provide the capillaries and higher blood hemoglobin concentration that supply your walking muscles with more oxygen. The more oxygen you can get to those working muscles, the higher the percentage of fat you'll burn during your marathon. And that's the key to breaking through or eliminating "the wall" (Chapter 25).

After you've developed sufficient endurance to get through the marathon, intervals, tempo work and long sub-threshold workouts will improve your speed and conditioning, which will get you through the marathon *faster*. Added to the mix are your easy days, which allow you to recover from the hard workouts, and help to improve your overall endurance.

When you do each type of workout is important. But actually *doing* the workouts is the most important thing. You can have the best training schedule in the world, but if it doesn't fit your lifestyle, it won't do you any good at all. Everybody has different goals and a different starting point, so the path you take may not be the same as anybody else's. With that in mind, the following schedules should be used as a starting point; a guide, not scripture. They're designed to give you the most bang out of the least amount of work. There are plenty of hard workouts to make you stronger, with enough rest to prevent fatigue from overtraining. But again, everybody is different: Some days you may be too tired or not have the time to do a particular workout. That's okay. Let your body tell you what it can and can not do. Missing a few workouts will not keep you from walking a great marathon. But at all cost, try to get that long day in every week, even if you have to switch days to do so. Then make sure you walk at least 30 to 45 minutes on at least two other days during the week to help you to retain the endurance gained during your long workouts. If you have more time to train, great—go longer. If you only have a few minutes to train, it's still worthwhile to get out and do *something*. If time is limited do less, but go faster. If you get in those three workouts, you'll finish the marathon. If you can add a few faster workouts during the week, like intervals, tempo workouts, or even an occasional 5K race, you'll finish the marathon *faster*.

Tapering

Once you've done your mileage build-up and completed several 18- to 20-mile walks, the real work is done. About three weeks before the race you'll "sharpen" by cutting your mileage back by anywhere from 1/3 to 2/3 of your normal workload to give your body a break from the long stuff and to work a bit more on marathon goal pace. This is your *taper* period. The goal of a taper is to ensure that you're well rested, but also to make sure you're "sharp" and fast. Your schedule should stay pretty much the same, but with less mileage and maybe a little bit more intensity (that means faster walking).

Your main objectives in the weeks before the race are physical and mental rest, and glycogen storage, but you also need to keep active enough to retain fitness and flexibility. *Too much* rest can leave you feeling flat and sluggish, but it's better to err on the side of doing too little rather than too much in the last few weeks. One of the biggest mistakes first-time marathoners make is trying to do too much too late. Whatever training you've done is "in there." You can't do a whole lot to improve your fitness in the week before the marathon, but you can beat yourself up and make yourself overtired and overtrained by trying to "catch up" on missed training.

A taper is just what it sounds like: a gradually tapering decrease in weekly mileage rather than a sudden drop. Most walkers will cut their weekly mileage by about one third the first week of the taper, then gradually drop down to about one half of their normal weekly mileage the week before the marathon. Others will cut back by as much as two thirds in the week before the race. I don't recommend dropping back that much because it violates one of the primary principles of marathon training: Don't do anything drastically different immediately before your race. You never know what effect such a drastic reduction will have on your body. Maybe you'll feel fine, but maybe you'll gain five pounds because your body is used to burning a lot more calories during the week. You never know.

For better or worse, whatever training you've done in the months before the marathon will rise to the top on race day—but only if you allow it to. You need to have faith in your conditioning going into the race. Don't undermine your training by doing too much in the last few weeks. So do cut back a bit, just don't cut back too much or make any drastic changes in your training program.

Rules of the road

As mentioned earlier, the following schedules will get you to the marathon fit and ready to go. But there are many paths to success. Your goals, your current level of conditioning, the amount of time you have to train, and the evil hand of genetics will all play a role in the exact nuts and bolts of how you will train for your marathon, and also in how well you will adapt to that training. Bad weather, job and family commitments, fatigue and other factors may prevent you from completing every workout exactly as it is written. And that's perfectly alright. Just try to make sure you don't cut too many corners, and try to do everything you can to consistently get yourself through those long walks.

If you're training for your first marathon, you should follow the beginner's schedule, regardless of any time goal you may have. You need to build strength before you can handle speed work and other elements of the more advanced schedules. If you have already completed at least one marathon and you want to try mixing some spurts of racewalking technique into your training and racing, you're ready to follow the intermediate schedule. You should only follow the advanced schedule if you've completed at least one marathon *and* you've been racewalking (as opposed to "regular" walking) for at least six months.

If you do not currently walk for exercise, you'll need to build up to the point where you can walk at least 30 minutes per day, three to five days per week, with a long walk that gradually increases to 90 minutes one day per week. Add no more than 15 minutes to the duration of your current longest walk during the week. If you are not walking at all now, allow six weeks to get up to 90 minutes: (6 x 15 = 90). At that point you can move on to week 1 of the beginner's schedule.

One final note: If you are part of a marathon training team or have your own coach, all bets are off. I hate to say it, but having someone there to guide your day-to-day training is always preferable to following a schedule printed in a book—even this one. By all means, discuss these schedules with your coach, but stick with his or her recommendations.

The following are my "secret codes" that will help you to decipher the training schedules:

★ These are your "must do" workouts. If you can't fit the workout in on the scheduled day, fit it into your week any way you can.

10-20-10 (or similar) These are tempo workouts. 10-20-10 means do an easy ten-minute warm-up, twenty minutes at tempo pace (half-marathon to 10K pace), then an easy ten-minute cool-down. It's okay to substitute a 5K to 10K race on these days. Just don't push *too* hard.

30-60 (or similar) This means walk anywhere from 30 to 60 minutes, usually at an easy pace.

60+ (or similar) Walk 60 minutes—or more if time allows.

Advanced The advanced schedule makes the assumption that you've already completed at least one marathon, and you've been using racewalking technique in training and in 5K and 10K races for at least six months. If you choose the advanced schedule, most or all of your marathon training will be done using racewalking technique.

A. Temp An acceleration tempo workout. After a complete warm up, then you'll start walking at your distance workout pace, but then gradually build up to your goal marathon pace or faster by the end of the workout.

Beginner This schedule is designed for the first-time marathoner, but it assumes that you are currently walking for exercise or can successfully complete an easy 90-minute walk. The goal is to get you ready to comfortably finish a marathon, at a pace somewhere between three and four miles per hour.

Economy Economy intervals are short, fast intervals with relatively long recoveries. Beginners will just walk very fast using their usual technique. More advanced walkers will use racewalking technique, aiming for their 5K race pace or slightly faster. Always do a complete warm-up before even thinking about doing this or any other fast workout! An example is a "6x200m" or "6x1 min" workout, which indicates six fast 200-meter or 1-minute intervals with about 200-meters (or two-minutes) of very easy walking to allow recovery between each fast interval.

EZ That's easy, it means "easy." On easy days you can either walk the prescribed amount of time, or do some easy cross-training like swimming, biking or roller-blading for a similar amount of time. But easy means easy! Pushing too hard on these days will detract from the quality of your hard days and will also keep you from fully recovering from those hard workouts. If in doubt, err on the side of doing too little rather than too much.

FTLK This is a "fartlek" workout. Fartlek is a Swedish word meaning "speed play." For our purposes, these are easyish walks, interrupted by one- to two-minute bursts of faster walking, perhaps using racewalking technique, or by walking fast up every hill if you train on a hilly course. Don't worry about when or how many bursts to do, just throw in a fast spurt whenever you feel like it.

Goal pace Whatever the workout, it should be walked at the same pace that you expect to walk your marathon. These are your so-called long sub-threshold workouts. Keep in mind it may take several long training walks before you begin to get a realistic idea of what your marathon pace will be.

Hrs Hours, as in "5 hrs." that means I want you to walk for 5 hours—ouch!

Intermediate The intermediate schedule assumes that you have already successfully completed at least one prior marathon, whether using racewalking or "regular" technique. If you are using the intermediate schedule, you can begin using racewalking technique by adding one- to two-minute bursts of racewalking technique every five or ten minutes during your long and easy days.

M Meters.

Mi Miles.

Mins Minutes.

Push Push the pace, usually down to half-marathon race pace—fast, but not crazy fast.

S Seconds, as in "+ 4 x :30s fast" which means walk 30 seconds fast, rest for a minute or so, then do it again three more times.

Tempo Tempo workout. See 10-20-10.

Thresh Lactate threshold intervals. Sounds scary, but they're really not all that bad. These are relatively "slow" intervals—at about 10K race pace rather than all-out—for a distance of 800 to 3,000 meters (about one half mile to two miles). Rests are on the order of one to three minutes.

W/ With.

X Times. As in "8x400." That means walk 400 meters at about 5K race pace (fast but not all-out), then recover for about two minutes (or 200 meters) of very easy walking, repeated eight times.

Beginner—6 ½ – 8 hour marathon

Week	M	T ★	W	Th ★	F	Sat	Sun ★
1	Off	Economy: 6x1 min	Off or EZ 30 min	Tempo: 10-10-10	EZ 30-45 minutes	Off or EZ 30 min	2 hrs. easy
2	Off	Economy: 6x1 min	Off or EZ 30 min	Tempo: 10-10-10	EZ 30-45 minutes	Off or EZ 30-45 min	2¼ hrs. easy
3	Off	Economy: 8x1 min	Off or EZ 30-45 min	Tempo: 10-10-10	EZ 45-60 minutes	Off or EZ 30-45 min	2 hrs. easy
4	Off	Economy: 8x1 min	Off or EZ 30-45 min	Tempo: 10-10-10	EZ 45-60 minutes	Off or EZ 30-45 min	2½ hrs. easy
5	Off	Economy: 10x1 min	Off or EZ 30-45 min	Tempo: 10-10-10	EZ 45-60 minutes	Off or EZ 30-45 min	3 hrs. easy
6	Off	Economy: 10x1 min	Off or EZ 30-45 min	Tempo: 10-20-10	EZ 45-60 minutes	Off or EZ 30-45 min	2½ hrs. easy
7	Off	Economy: 12x1 min	Off or EZ 45-60 min	Tempo: 10-20-10	EZ 60 minutes	Off or EZ 30-45 min	3½ hrs. easy
8	Off	Economy: 12x1 min	Off or EZ 45-60 min	Tempo: 10-20-10	EZ 60 minutes	Off or EZ 30-45 min	3 hrs. easy
9	Off	Economy: 6x2 min	Off or EZ 45-60 min	Tempo: 10-20-10	EZ 60 minutes	Off or EZ 30-45 min	4 hrs. easy
10	Off	60 min FTLK	Off or EZ 45-60 min	Tempo: 10-30-10	EZ 60 minutes	Off or EZ 30-45 min	3 hrs. easy
11	Off	Economy: 8x2 min	Off or EZ 60 min	Tempo: 10-30-10	EZ 60 minutes	Off or EZ 30-45 min	4½ hrs. easy
12	Off	60 min FTLK	Off or EZ 60 min	Tempo: 10-30-10	EZ 60 minutes	Off or EZ 30-45 min	3 hrs. @ Goal Pace
13	Off	Economy: 10x2 min	Off or EZ 60 min	Tempo: 10-30-10	EZ 60 minutes	Off or EZ 30-45 min	5 hrs. easy
14	Off	60 min FTLK	Off or EZ 60 min	Tempo: 10-40-10	EZ 60 minutes	Off or EZ 30-45 min	3 hrs. @ Goal Pace
15	Off	Economy: 12x2 min	Off or EZ 45 min	Tempo: 10-40-10	EZ 60 minutes	Off or EZ 30-45 min	5 hrs. easy
16	Off	60 min FTLK	Off or EZ 30-45 min	Tempo: 10-40-10	EZ 60 minutes	Off or EZ 30-45 min	3 EZ, push 3rd hour
17	Off	Economy: 8x2 min	Off or EZ 30-45 min	Tempo: 10-30-10	Off or EZ 30-45 min	Off or EZ 30-45 min	2 hrs. @ Goal Pace
18	Off	20 min FTLK	Off or EZ 30 min	Tempo: 10-10-10	Off or EZ 20 min	EZ 20min + 4 x :30s	**Marathon!**

Intermediate—5 ½ - 6 ½ hours

Week	M	T ★	W	Th ★	F	Sat	Sun ★
1	Off	45 min FTLK	Off or EZ 30 min	Tempo: 10-10-10	EZ 30-45 minutes	Off or EZ 30 min	8 miles easy
2	Off	45 min FTLK	Off or EZ 30 min	Tempo: 10-10-10	EZ 30-45 minutes	Off or EZ 30 min	9 miles easy
3	Off	60 min FTLK	Off or EZ 30-45 min	Tempo: 10-10-10	EZ 45-60 minutes	Off or EZ 30-45 min	8 miles easy
4	Off	60 min FTLK	Off or EZ 30-45 min	Tempo: 10-10-10	EZ 45-60 minutes	Off or EZ 30-45 min	10 miles easy
5	Off	60 min FTLK	Off or EZ 30-45 min	Tempo: 10-20-10	EZ 45-60 minutes	Off or EZ 30-45 min	12 miles easy
6	Off	60 min FTLK	Off or EZ 30-45 min	Tempo: 10-20-10	EZ 45-60 minutes	Off or EZ 30-45 min	10 mi. @ goal pace
7	Off	60 min FTLK	Off or EZ 30-45 min	Tempo: 10-30-10	EZ 60 minutes	Off or EZ 30-45 min	14 miles easy
8	Off	60 min FTLK	Off or EZ 30-45 min	Tempo: 10-30-10	EZ 60 minutes	Off or EZ 30-45 min	12 mi. @ goal pace
9	Off	60 min FTLK	Off or EZ 30-45 min	Tempo: 10-30-10	EZ 60 minutes	Off or EZ 30-45 min	16 miles easy
10	Off	Economy: 10x200m	Off or EZ 30-45 min	Tempo: 10-40-10	EZ 60 minutes	Off or EZ 30-45 min	12 mi. @ goal pace
11	Off	60 min FTLK	Off or EZ 30-45 min	Tempo: 10-40-10	EZ 60 minutes	Off or EZ 30-45 min	18 miles easy
12	Off	Economy: 12x200m	Off or EZ 30-45 min	Tempo: 10-40-10	EZ 60 minutes	Off or EZ 30-45 min	12 mi. @ goal pace
13	Off	60 min FTLK	Off or EZ 30-45 min	Tempo: 10-40-10	EZ 60 minutes	Off or EZ 30-45 min	20 miles easy
14	Off	Economy: 12x200m	Off or EZ 30-45 min	Tempo: 10-40-10	EZ 60 minutes	Off or EZ 30-45 min	12 mi. @ goal pace
15	Off	60 min FTLK	Off or EZ 30-45 min	Tempo: 10-40-10	EZ 60 minutes	Off or EZ 30-45 min	20 miles easy
16	Off	Economy: 8x400m	Off or EZ 30-45 min	Tempo: 10-40-10	EZ 60 minutes	Off or EZ 30-45 min	12 miles push last 4
17	Off	40 min FTLK	Off or EZ 30-45 min	Tempo: 10-30-10	Off or EZ 30-45 min	Off or EZ 30-45 min	8 Miles @ goal pace
18	Off	20 min FTLK	Off or EZ 30 min	Tempo: 10-10-10	Off or EZ 20 min	EZ 20min + 4 x :30s	**Marathon!**

Advanced—Under 5 ½ hours

Week	M	T ★	W	Th ★	F	Sat	Sun ★
1	Off	Economy: 6x200m	EZ 30-45 minutes	Tempo: 10-10-10	EZ 30-45 minutes	Off or EZ 30 min	8 miles easy
2	Off	Economy: 6x200m	EZ 30-45 minutes	Tempo: 10-10-10	EZ 30-45 minutes	Off or EZ 30 min	9 miles easy
3	Off	Economy: 8x200m	EZ 45-60 minutes	Tempo: 10-20-10	EZ 45-60 minutes	Off or EZ 30-45 min	8 miles easy
4	Off	Economy: 8x200m	EZ 45-60 minutes	Tempo: 10-20-10	EZ 45-60 minutes	Off or EZ 30-45 min	10 miles easy
5	Off	Economy: 10x200m	EZ 45-60 minutes	A. Temp: 45	EZ 45-60 minutes	Off or EZ 30-45 min	12 miles easy
6	Off	Economy: 10x200m	EZ 45-60 minutes	Tempo: 10-30-10	EZ 45-60 minutes	Off or EZ 30-45 min	10 mi. @ goal pace
7	Off	Economy: 12x200m	EZ 60 minutes	A. Temp: 45 min	EZ 60 minutes	Off or EZ 30-45 min	14 miles easy
8	Off	Economy: 12x200m	EZ 60 minutes	Tempo: 10-30-10	EZ 60 minutes	Off or EZ 30-45 min	12 mi. @ goal pace
9	Off	Economy: 6x400m	EZ 60 minutes	A. Temp: 60 min	EZ 60 minutes	Off or EZ 30-45 min	16 miles easy
10	Off	Economy: 6x400m	EZ 60 minutes	Tempo: 10-40-10	EZ 60 minutes	Off or EZ 30-45 min	12 mi. @ goal pace
11	Off	Economy: 8x400m	EZ 60 minutes	A. Temp: 60 min	EZ 60 minutes	Off or EZ 30-45 min	18 miles easy
12	Off	Thresh. 4x800m	EZ 60 minutes	Tempo: 10-40-10	EZ 60 minutes	Off or EZ 30-45 min	12 mi. @ goal pace
13	Off	Thresh. 6x800m	EZ 60 minutes	A. Temp: 75 min	EZ 60 minutes	Off or EZ 30-45 min	20 miles easy
14	Off	Thresh. 6x800m	EZ 60 minutes	Tempo: 10-60-5	EZ 60 minutes	Off or EZ 30-45 min	12 mi. @ goal pace
15	Off	Thresh: 3x1600m	EZ 60 minutes	A. Temp: 75 min	EZ 60 minutes	Off or EZ 30-45 min	20 miles easy
16	Off	Economy: 8x400m	EZ 60 minutes	Tempo: 10-40-10	EZ 60 minutes	Off or EZ 30-45 min	15 mi. push last 4
17	Off	Thresh: 3x1600m	Off or EZ 30-45 min	A. Temp: 45 min	Off or EZ 30-45 min	Off or EZ 30-45 min	8 Miles @ goal pace
18	Off	Economy: 4x400m	Off or EZ 30 min	Tempo: 10-10-10	Off or EZ 20 min	EZ 20min + 4 x :30s	**Marathon!**

Chapter 15

A Few Words on Overtraining

Although you definitely need to work hard to become a good marathon walker, it is possible to overdo it. Don't be a bonehead—it's always much better to go into a marathon marginally undertrained than to show up at the starting line overtrained. I've never had a problem getting through a marathon that I didn't feel completely ready for. The only ones I've ever had trouble with were the ones I've tried to "train through" by not cutting back on my mileage the week before the race. And those crashes were ugly!

Steady improvements in fitness come from allowing your body to adapt to reasonable stresses. Consistent, intelligent training leads to success; overstress without recovery does nothing but make you tired. Doing too much will eventually lead to illness, injury and sub-par marathon performances.

Over racing

"Over racing" is as bad or worse than over training—especially when it comes to marathons. It generally takes about one month to fully recover from a hard marathon, even if you've trained properly for it. And it could take much longer. It's easy to get excited and catch the "marathon bug," but you really shouldn't attempt more than two or three marathons per year. Injuries or mental "burn-out" will eventually catch up to you and derail your training and racing performance.

You may decide to race some shorter races like 5Ks, 10Ks and half-marathons as part of your marathon training, but again, try to avoid racing too often. If you must compete frequently, don't treat every race like it's the Olympics. You can't be "up" for every competition—if you try to do so you'll walk yourself into the ground. If you're lucky enough to have frequent races on your local calendar pick the ones that are the most important to you and key for them. Use the others as tempo walks, but don't push too hard! Hold yourself back by walking these "tempo" races about 30 seconds per mile slower than you could go if you were racing all-out—or even slower if you're scheduled for a long walk the next day.

If you don't have the self-control to hold back, but still want to be a part of the race, volunteer to work registration or results. But leave those racing shoes at home! Whenever I help out at a local race I always make sure I leave my racing shoes at home so I won't be tempted to take off when I hear the sound of the starting gun. Of course there's no guarantee that I won't at least *try* to race—I've "blown-out" a few pair of Tevas that way, but having a flip-flop explode into shreds 20 meters into a 5K is usually enough to make me stop racing, so I guess the strategy works.

Warning signs

As soon as you start feeling overtrained, you need to take a day or two off before it's too late. But how do you know when you're overtrained? Signs of overtraining are:

- sudden unexplained weight loss

- personality changes like irritability or loss of enthusiasm

- heavy legs or sore muscles

- changes in sleeping habits or insomnia

- loss of appetite or excessive thirst

- diminished sex drive

- swollen glands

96

- an unusually high morning pulse rate.

Of course these symptoms also sound a lot like malaria, rabies, and a variety of other maladies, but even if it *is* rabies or some nasty tropical disease, you should *still* take the day off.

Use your training log (Chapter 18) to gauge how well you're recovering from your training. Weigh yourself, and take resting pulse rate every morning—if your morning heart rate is more than 10% higher than usual or if you're losing weight *too* suddenly, take an easy day—or better yet, a day off—no matter what your schedule says. You're probably fatigued, dehydrated and on the verge of a breakdown. Or maybe it's just a touch of that West Nile Fever virus that's been going around...

Great Walking Marathons:
Honolulu Marathon, Honolulu, HI

The Honolulu Marathon is an event of extremes. It's easily one of the world's largest marathons, with more than 30,000 entrants. And Honolulu is certainly one of the most attractive marathon destinations—a vibrant city within a tropical paradise replete with palm trees, beautiful beaches, tropical rain forests, waterfalls and lots of "aloha" spirit. The course is hilly, and of course, heat and humidity are unavoidable, but if you're willing to sacrifice a blazing fast race time, Honolulu is unquestionably one of the most unforgettable places to walk a marathon.

More than 20,000 Japanese tourists enter the race—many of them walking or running with little or no prior training. So you'll have plenty of company on the course even if you aren't the speediest of walkers. And you'll also feel no pressure to get to the party in Kapiolani Park in a hurry, since the course stays open until the last finisher comes home. But if you do push the pace, there are great racewalk awards for the top finishers, and even if you don't take home one of the division winner awards, all finishers take home cowry shell lei finishers' medals.

The 5:00 a.m. start at Ala Moana Beach Park is made somewhat easier for mainlanders by the time zone change, so get there early. With such a huge crowd packed into a relatively narrow starting area, it'll take latecomers a long while to cross the starting line after the howitzer blast and fireworks show start the race—and the marathon doesn't yet use the chip system to make up the time difference.

The course takes you past tourist spots like Honolulu Harbor, Aloha Tower, Chinatown, Iolani Palace, and the gilded statue of King Kamehameha before you cross the Ala Wai Canal into Waikiki and Kapiolani Park. After seven miles of dead-flat roads, you may be lulled into thinking you have an easy morning ahead of you. But once you turn out of the park you're on the road up Diamond Head, and the hills begin—just in time for the road to start heating up in the morning sun. After cruising down the other side of Diamond Head there are miles of flats—but no shade—on the Kalanianaole Highway before you return to the hills just after 20 miles. Another climb up and down Diamond Head and it's a flat stretch to the finish in Kapiolani Park. It may not be the easiest of courses, but the crowds and other walkers are supportive, the aid stations are plentiful, and once you finish, Waikiki Beach awaits you!

Chapter 16

Care and Feeding of Walking Injuries

I'm still waiting for the tabloids to report the <u>real</u> government cover up: not the Elvis on Mars thing, or the pregnant crocodile-baby. I want them to expose The Big Lie: "Walking: the Injury-Free Sport!" Walkers certainly do sustain a whole lot fewer injuries than runners, that much is true. But any activity taken to an extreme (and yes, walking a marathon *is* an extreme thing to do!) can lead to injuries. That doesn't necessarily mean you'll get injured—most walkers get through their training and marathons just fine. And even if you do wind up with an "owie," that certainly doesn't mean an end to your marathoning hopes. But you should be aware that even though you've wisely chosen to *walk* your marathon, injuries *can* still happen.

I've been lucky enough over the years to train through most of my injuries. But I have had my fair share of nasties that have required medical attention, so I've seen a good number of doctors. Most sports medicine specialists receive fine training in our medical schools, and receive lots of great on-the-job training treating a daily throng of synchronized swimmers, horse shoe pitchers, dog mushers and limbo dancers. But the problem with doctors is that they work in generalities: If a doctor works with a lot of basketball players or skiers, a torn meniscus is probably a reasonable guess as the source of medial knee pain. Likewise, a sprain may be a likely diagnosis for a soccer player, and chondromalacia is fairly common among runners. Unfortunately most doctors haven't seen very many marathon walkers and aren't sure what kinds of assumptions they should make.

Origins and insertions

I've found that marathon walkers suffer relatively few serious injuries, but nearly all the injuries they do suffer are overuse injuries rather than traumatic ones like joint sprains and muscle tears. Tendonitis of the knees (iliotibial or sartorial), feet (plantar fasciitis or peroneal-cuboid syndrome), shins ("shin splints," anterior compartment syndrome or posterior tibial myositis/tendonitis), or of the Achilles tendons are all common overuse injuries in walkers. Bursitis of the hips or knees is also fairly common.

Tendonitis is very easily treated if you catch it early: Some Advil, ice, and a little stretching and massage therapy and you're usually on your way. The problem, though, is that tendonitis usually comes on slowly, getting a little bit worse after every hard workout. The trick with treating tendonitis is to remember just what tendons are: They're tough fibrous sheaths that connect muscles to bones. Fortunately, 99% of the time there's nothing seriously wrong with the tendon itself, it's simply being abused by a tight muscle. As the muscle shortens, it pulls at its origin and insertion points (at the tendons and fascial sheaths) and gets a little inflamed.

Similarly, bursitis is the inflammation of a bursa (a fluid-filled sac formed in areas of friction). As the muscles tighten, friction around the joints increases and the bursae are irritated. The only way to release the strain or irritation of the tendon or bursa is to lengthen the muscle by stretching it. It's a lot like somebody pulling your hair: The hair itself doesn't hurt, it's the insertion point at the scalp that's making you scream. Anti-inflammatories, pain-killers, ice, and thinking happy thoughts may all help, but eliminating that "pulling" by stretching or massaging is ultimately the only way to make the pain go away.

The quick fix

Athletes are often seduced by a quick-fix, Band-Aid approach to sports medicine: Rest, use ice and aspirin, and the pain will go away. All true to some extent, but these approaches attack the symptom and not the cause. The pain may be in the tendon or bursa, but the root cause is the weak, tight, neglected muscle. Long-term treatment for these injuries must begin with isolation of the muscle or muscles involved. In many cases you'll notice discomfort and tightness in muscles that lie far from the injured area. Don't ignore these sensations! These muscles could be the source of the irritated tendons or bursae. My first serious bout with tendonitis involved the insertion of my iliotibial band at the outside of my right knee. I felt a little tightness on the outside of my right hip as well, but thought nothing of it, since it was never very painful and was so far away from the hurting knee.

The injury eventually forced me to take two months off, and to pull out of the 1987 World Racewalking Cup. Whenever I tried to return to training, the knee would hurt just as much as it did at the time of the initial injury. Two months of rest did nothing to cure the knee because I failed to attack the tight hip muscles and iliotibial band. The treatment that finally cured me involved having a physical therapist dig at the "necrotic" scar tissue in my hip and thigh with the back end of a screwdriver to release the muscle and tendon, and then learning how to ward off further flare-ups with a sensible stretching routine. I recently had one of my marathon walkers come to me with exactly the same injury: a textbook case of iliotibial tendonitis that was misdiagnosed by her doctor as a torn meniscus. I showed her how to stretch the I.T. band (Chapter 12) and she was back on the roads almost immediately.

If you wind up with an injury that involves pain in an isolated area—usually at a joint like the knee, ankle or the metatarsal bones of the feet, chances are you have tendonitis. Treat the symptoms immediately— use ice and anti-inflammatories to reduce swelling, and take a few days off if you have to, but then work on the root cause of the pain. Rest without rehabilitation will not make the problem go away. You need to massage and stretch the muscles that are pulling on the affected tendon. You may be able to feel which muscles are involved by "palpating" all the muscles around the injured area and working your way out. A good anatomy book or a massage therapist can help you to zero in on the affected muscles. If you still can't find the cause and the pain keeps you off your feet for more than a week, then you'll probably have to call a sports medicine doctor or physical therapist.

After the inflammation subsides you'll need to spend some time strengthening the root-cause of the tendonitis, which is almost always a muscle imbalance, or weak muscles in general. For tendonitis of the feet and lower legs I've had a lot of success from simply doing a lot of barefoot walking, and walking in sandals to strengthen those muscles. For just about everything else I go straight to the weight room.

An ounce of prevention is worth two in the bush (or something like that...) If you feel tight and beat up the day after a hard workout, stay inside and stretch! Attack those tight muscles before they turn into debilitating injuries.

Rehabilitation

Stretching is an important first step in injury recovery, but gains in flexibility will be short-lived if the involved muscles are weak and atrophied. Strength training is critical in injury rehabilitation or preventative care. Whether using free weights, weight machines, elastic devices or isometric exercises, the involved muscles should be isolated in such a way as to ensure that they are being worked through a range of motion that mimics the walking action as closely as possible. This may involve a good deal of improvisation with weight machines, or experimentation with postural changes until the perfect position is found.

During rehabilitation, resistance should be just enough to cause minor fatigue without causing pain in the injured area. As strength improves, work up to three sets of 10 to 12 repetitions. Always allow 48 hours for recovery between sessions—three days of weight training per week is optimal.

I've said a lot about tendonitis-type injuries, but there are a number of other, less serious maladies that may befall you during your marathon training and racing. You should be able to take care of these minor problems easily, without missing any training. Among these are:

- **Blisters.** Blisters form in places where the skin is rubbed repeatedly—usually by an ill-fitting shoe. Many walkers rub Vaseline on their feet before training to prevent blisters, but doing so may also cause your feet to slide around too much, which could cause worse blisters or other problems. Double-layered socks work really well for some walkers, but others find that these socks may actually *cause* blisters because they allow the foot to slide around more than they would in a single-thickness pair of socks. Experiment with different sock thicknesses to see what works best for you, and never go out on a long workout in a pair of shoes or socks that you haven't first tested on several shorter workouts. Perhaps the most direct solution is to spray your feet with a little bit of aerosol anti-perspirant before you walk. It prevents your feet from sweating so they don't slide around in your shoes as much. It may even make your feet smell better. If you already have a blister, cover it with a Band-Aid or mole skin. If the blister is big enough to interfere with your walking the next day, I say pop it with a sterilized needle then apply some antiseptic and cover it with a Band-Aid or sterile gauze. (Although Ms. Kennedy, my old high school nurse, is apt to be very upset when she reads that.) I find that if I don't drain the fluid, the blister eventually tears open and then things get *really* ugly. Eventually, frequently blistered areas will thicken, forming a hard, scaly callous—so at least you have that to look forward to.

- **Black toenails.** These ugly buggers will really impress your friends. Black toenails are formed when blood collects in a blister under a traumatized toenail. Although black toenails are most frequently caused by tight shoes, they can also form when your shoes are too large, so you're damned if you do, and damned if you don't. The nail will eventually "die" and fall off, but if it really hurts you may want to see a podiatrist who'll pop a hole in the nail with a hot paper clip—a high-tech solution I now do myself for about 85 bucks less than the D.P.M. version. Keeping your toenails clipped will help prevent them from recurring, as will cutting a small hole in your shoe above the affected nail.

- **Sore shins.** Most walkers and racewalkers suffer from sore shins in the first few weeks of their marathon training. While many runners suffer from a more serious condition known as "shin splints," in most cases walkers sustain nothing more than muscle soreness in their shins. Not to say that it doesn't hurt—it does. But after a few weeks or sometimes months of training, the shin muscles are strengthened and the pain goes away. If your shins burn after a few minutes of walking, stop and massage them. Taking ibuprofen (Advil) before your walks and icing afterwards will also help, as will changing to a shoe with a lower heel and shortening your stride.

- **Side stitches.** Not an injury, *per se,* but they can be pretty painful, nonetheless. A side stitch is a temporary pain in the side, below or under the rib cage, caused by an insufficient oxygen supply to the diaphragm—a sheath of muscle below the lungs that helps you breath. If you get a stitch while training, bend sideways away from the side that hurts, while massaging the area. The theory behind the cure is that you're trying to get oxygen into the area—although simply stopping your walk to do the stretch probably does as much good as the stretch itself. Eventually, as you get fitter, the oxygen supply to the diaphragm increases and the stitches stop occurring.

- **Chaffing.** Chaffing is a nasty rash that occurs when you rub two areas of skin together 140 or more times per minute while you walk. Skin rubbing against a wet cotton T-shirt, or against a seam in your shorts or top can also become chaffed. Chaffing most commonly occurs when you're dehydrated—after you've stopped sweating and your skin is left covered with a film of sticky salt crystals. Staying hydrated will help, as will wearing half-tights under your shorts, or avoiding 100% cotton T-shirts—depending on where the chaffing occurs. Losing weight will also help—enough said. Many walkers solve the problem by smearing the affected areas with Vaseline before or during training or racing. I find that rubbing a little hair conditioner on the area in the shower, then rinsing it off, before my long walks lubricates the skin just enough to prevent any problems without the gross feeling of Vaseline on your skin. Body Glide is a new roll-on product that's also very effective.

- **Lower back pain.** Many lower back problems in marathon walkers are caused either by poor posture or by bad walking technique. Bending forward at the waist while walking, and overstriding seem to be the most common technique-induced causes of chronic back pain. The treatment, then, is obvious: Straighten up and shorten your stride. Training too much on crowned roads, where one foot strikes the ground lower than the other, is another route to back pain. Finding a flatter walking surafce may help. In addition, you may also want to try warm baths, moist heat packs, massage, chiropractic care or even acupuncture. Weak and/or tight hamstring, hip or abdominal muscles may also contribute to back problems, so stretching and strengthening these areas may also be helpful.

A SCARIER Way to Treat Injuries

Although the RICE method—Rest, Ice, Compression, Elevation—is somewhat effective in treating walking injuries, it leaves out a few important elements: Stretching, Rehydration and Anti-inflammatories. Walkers with injuries shouldn't stop at RICE, but should try something SCARIER: Stretch, Compress, Anti-inflammatories, Rehydrate, Ice, Elevate, Rest.

- **Stretch** the muscles. Most walking injuries are tendonitis or bursitis-type injuries. The root cause of these injuries is tight muscles that "pull" on tendon insertions. Stretching the tight muscles will relieve the strain on the tendon insertions.

- **Compress** the sore spots to push out excess fluids. Also compress—by massaging—the tight muscles to work out any knots, and to break up scar tissue.

- **Anti-inflammatories** like ibuprofen (Advil) or Aleve will further reduce swelling.

- **Rehydrate** those dried out, beef-jerky muscles. Muscles are 75% water—a dry muscle is a tight muscle. DRINK!

- **Ice** for ten minutes on, ten off for 30 minutes after training. A bag of frozen peas is the best ice pack known to modern medical science.

- **Elevate** the feet whenever possible. Elevation will allow fluid to drain out of the swollen areas.

- **Rest** as a last resort. Unless the injury is very serious you should try to continue walking, but take it very easy and cut back on your mileage by about 50%. Warming up the muscles by doing some easy walking will allow you to get a better stretch, and will circulate lots of healing blood to the area. I don't think of it as real training, but as "therapeutic walking."

Coming back from an injury

Patience is the keyword when returning from a prolonged injury layoff. Don't rush things. Again, most walking injuries are *overuse* injuries. Your body is trying to tell you something: "Take it easy, Dummy!"

A certain amount of "detraining" will set in after any layoff. Speed is the first thing to go, but before long endurance is also degraded. The good news is that it takes a lot less time to return to top form than it took to get there in the first place, so don't rush things.

I've often been told that it takes two weeks to come back from every week off from training, but I've found that it seems to take two weeks to return from *any* extended layoff. If I've been off for a month, the first two weeks back will feel like garbage, but then things will always "click" suddenly after about two weeks.

One rule of thumb that I do believe, however, is that you shouldn't do any hard training after a layoff until you've gotten at least as much easy training in as you've lost. If you were off for two weeks, don't even think about doing speed work, tempo work or hard distance work until you've gotten at least two good weeks under your belt after the break. If you were off for six weeks, get in six weeks of rebuilding training before returning to the hard or really long stuff. That doesn't mean you can't do any long or hard walking. It just means that you should allow yourself the full six weeks to get back to where you were before the layoff.

When coming back from an injury it's very important to look at the big picture. Your goal is to finish a marathon, and you will not be able to achieve that goal if you show up at the starting line with a significant injury. You *can* finish the marathon if you've lost several weeks—or even months—of training. One of my athletes wanted to make sure she could handle the rigors of marathon training before agreeing to sign up to train for the 1999 Chicago Marathon. So she walked a 10-mile workout in brand new shoes a week before our training program began—just to see if you could do it. Predictably, she wound up with an injury. She never did get around to training with the team, but by the time the marathon rolled around she had recovered from the injury and was pain-free. That first 10-mile walk was her only walk over three miles, and yet—against our advice to wait for another marathon—she finished in Chicago! You *can* finish a marathon without a lot of training. You won't set any records, and you stand a greater risk of hurting yourself during or after the marathon, but you can do it. On the other hand, you have almost no chance of finishing the race if you show up at the starting line hobbled by an injury. So if you do sustain an injury, don't rush your comeback!

Injuries almost always happen to "other people." But there is a reasonable chance that your marathon training may help you to unearth a previously undiscovered "weak link" in your anatomy. If it does, don't panic, but don't ignore it either. If you can determine the cause and get to work right away on treating the problem, your down time will be measured in days rather than weeks or months.

Heidi Hauch on:
Recovering From an Injury

Age: 43
Marathon PR: 4:21:17
Marathons Completed: Rock & Roll '98, Honolulu '98, Mayor's Midnight Sun '99, Disney '00, Valley of the Sun '01, Rock & Roll '01, Reggae '02.

Heidi started walking marathons in 1998 when she found out her 4-year-old nephew, Jack, was diagnosed with leukemia. After training with the Arizona Chapter of the Leukemia & Lymphoma Society's Team in Training program she walked the 1998 Rock & Roll Marathon with her sisters and was hooked.

Heidi says: "I wound up injuring my knee in November of 1999 after racing a 20K, a half-marathon and a 10K on successive weekends, all the while training for the Disney Marathon. In retrospect I guess I was asking my body to do too much without giving it enough rest. When my knee went I immediately began cross-training by biking and swimming but I didn't really do any kind of therapy to recover from the injury. On December 26th, two weeks before the Disney Marathon I realized it was sink or swim so I went out and did a 17-mile training walk. Then the next week I did 12 miles. The knee wasn't bad, but my coach still suggested I take it easy during the marathon. That plan went right out the window when the gun went off. Racewalking felt good and the knee didn't hurt at all until 13 miles. I won the racewalk division, PR'd, but wound up re-injuring the knee.

"After Disney I went to a series of doctors and physical therapists and we eventually figured out what was wrong and took care of the problem with stretching and strengthening exercises. I think it's really important to be as specific as possible with your doctor by giving him the what, where and when it hurts to help get the correct diagnosis of *why* it hurts. Finding out what is causing the problem is key, because then you can take the necessary steps to correct it. I had never really bothered stretching and strengthening before—I just reasoned that I'd always been really flexible and I was strengthening my walking muscles by walking. Then I found out my injury was being exacerbated by weak and unstretched areas. So, where I used to just lace 'em up and head out the door, I now incorporate a stretching and strengthening routine into my walking workout. It takes a bit more time, but it's well worth it to get off the injured list and back into the fun of walking!"

Chapter 17

Where to Walk

Now you know *how* to walk—how far, how fast, and with what kind of technique—but what about *where* to walk? If you're planning on doing a marathon, your training should simulate the conditions you're likely to experience in the race. But some people only walk on tracks, or on the treadmill at the local gym. It's okay to do some of your training in these "artificial" environments, but you really should try to walk on the roads as often as possible.

Safety first

Your personal safety is the most important consideration when choosing an outdoor training site. A bike path that's closed to automobile traffic is ideal, but if you don't have one nearby, you can still find good places to train in almost any city or town if you look around a bit. Park perimeter roads, quiet country roads, hiking trails, even fire roads and cemeteries can provide relatively automobile-free walking.

It's also a good idea to find courses that are populated by other walkers and runners. Having other people around can be a great motivator, but even more important, there's safety in numbers. If you live in a quieter area or can't find a place to train where other walkers congregate, and you can't find a two-legged walking partner, it's not a bad idea to walk with a dog.

If you can't find a completely automobile-free training venue, do what you can to be seen by drivers. Try to get out in daylight hours, and if that isn't possible, look for well-lit courses and wear light-colored or reflective clothing. Always face oncoming traffic and be prepared to get off the road in a hurry if a driver decides he doesn't want to move over for you. And don't wear headphones when walking. Music may help to pass the time, but you need to be aware of your surroundings at all times.

Headphones may prevent you from hearing a dangerous dog, person or automobile approaching you from behind.

Even if you don't wear headphones, you need to be alert when you're out training. I've escaped being run over on numerous occasions including one time in Georgia when a driver who had run me off the road actually turned around, drove back up the road, then turned around to try again. After another near-miss she got out of her van to yell at me for walking on the quiet country road where "only cars are supposed to be." When I stopped to argue with her she smacked me in the face. Better her hand than her bumper I guess.

I actually was hit by a car once while training in Ft. Lauderdale, Florida. Luckily the tiny old woman who plowed into me had slowed down considerably to take an illegal right turn at a red light (without stopping), so I was only slightly bruised when I wound up on the hood of her dandelion-yellow diesel behemoth. Valiantly navigating her Mercedes through town by looking out from under her steering wheel, she never did bother to stop—even after I tore the windshield wiper off the car while sliding off the hood.

Obviously being hit by a car should be your foremost concern, but you also need to be wary of the car's occupants. I've had numerous beer bottles thrown at me while training in Wisconsin and I once had several "D" batteries whiz by my head during a distance workout in New York's Central Park. But given the choice, I'd rather dodge a Duracel than a Dodge any day. Hopefully your training walks won't be as "interesting" as some of mine have been, but it only takes one drunk, psychotic or teen-age driver to put an end to your marathon training—or your life.

"Accidents" happen to those who don't anticipate them. Follow these rules of the road to keep your walks safe:

- **Always face traffic.** But keep in mind that facing traffic won't do you a bit of good if you—or the driver—are not paying attention. Try to make eye contact if possible so you can better judge what the driver is up to.

- **Never assume.** Drivers are not necessarily going to act logically (or legally) in a given situation. If you're going to assume anything, assume the worst. Don't cross in front of stopped cars whether the driver sees you or not, be very careful crossing side-streets, and of course, look both ways before crossing—if a car slows down as it approaches you, don't assume it's going to stop.

- **Wear light-colored or reflective clothing.** Assuming that most drivers aren't gunning for you, visible clothing will allow drivers to see you sooner. Of course bright clothing will also make you a more visible target if a driver actually is out to get you...

- **Don't play chicken.** Pedestrians have the right-of-way. This phrase tops the list of famous last words. Cars should yield to runners and walkers. Most will not. Don't let your sense of justice get you killed.

- **Avoid confrontation.** To paraphrase Forest Gump, drivers are like a box of chocolates—you never know what you're gonna get. The old woman who smacked me in Georgia could have just as likely been a big genetic mutant with a tire iron and a bad attitude. It's not necessarily a good idea to flip the bird to someone in control of 4,000 lbs. of fast moving iron and steel.

Specificity

Another consideration when choosing an outdoor training site is finding a course that will prepare you for the specific challenges of the marathon for which you are training. If a hilly marathon is in your plans, you should try to train on hills at least a few times per week. You walk with slightly different technique and use somewhat different muscles on hills, so walking solely on the flats won't fully prepare you for a hilly marathon. If you don't have any "real" hills in your area, long bridges or even parking garage ramps are viable substitutes. You can get a good hill workout by occasionally training on a treadmill set to a three to five percent incline, but your technique on the treadmill may not be the same as it is on the roads, so it's important to do at least some of your hill training outside.

Training on the roads will also get your legs used to the "crown" or "camber" of the road. The center of most roads is usually slightly higher than the edges so that rainwater will drain faster. So walking on a crowned road is a little like wearing a heel lift in only one shoe. You can eventually get used to it by training on such a road, but if you don't do enough on-the-road training ahead of time, you may injure yourself during your marathon when you are suddenly forced to contend with the crowned road.

Getting on track

An outdoor high school or college track is a great place to do your faster walking. You're assured a flat, usually smooth and forgiving surface, there are probably bathrooms and water nearby, and the track is a standard measured distance—in most cases 400 meters, or about 7 feet short of a quarter mile. (In lane one, that is… A few feet are added to that distance with every lane you move out from lane one. That's because you're walking around a bigger circle the further out from lane one you go.)

I prefer to do my distance training on the roads, but I head to the track for most of my economy and threshold interval workouts. Most tracks are open to the public and are quite popular with other walkers and runners. The school track team may "rule the roost" at certain times of the day, but any time the facility is not reserved for organized practices you have just as much right to be there as anyone else. Even so, it's important to follow the proper track etiquette. Specific rules may be posted at the track. If not, the following protocols are standard practice:

- **Warm-up in the outer lanes.** Both to limit wear and tear on the heavily-used innermost lanes and to keep out of the way of faster runners and walkers. Once you start the faster part of the workout it should be okay to move to lane one or two.

- **Walk single-file.** Especially when you are walking in the first few lanes. Faster walkers and runners passing from behind aren't going to mind going around you if you stay to the inside of the lane. But they might get irked if they have to move all the way out to lane three because you and your friends are taking up the whole track by walking four abreast.

- **Keep taking lefts.** If nobody else is in your lane it's not a bad idea to switch directions every once in a while to keep from overusing your "left turn muscles." But when other people are on the track, the preferred direction is counter-clockwise.

- **Look before you leap.** Never step onto the track, switch lanes, or stop suddenly without first looking to see if anyone is coming.

Treadmills

Although I certainly wouldn't recommend using them every day, a treadmill can be a valuable training tool when conditions outside are not conducive to quality training. I certainly prefer training outdoors, but for dangerous weather days—freezing rain or life-threatening heat and humidity—you can't beat 'em.

Treadmills can also be an effective change of pace if you live in a very flat, or an excessively hilly location. I coach many walkers in places like South Florida and New Orleans who don't have any hills on which to train. I have them set the treadmill to a reasonable grade of three to five percent for at least some of their workouts—enough of a grade to ensure a good hill workout, but not so much that their technique suffers.

If, on the other hand, walking in your neighborhood is more like a roller coaster ride than a workout, try heading indoors a few days per week for your marathon pace workouts or perhaps for your easy walks. The problem with *too many* hills is that you can't really get into a rhythm during your workouts. It helps to be able to maintain good race-specific technique when training—your technique can begin to suffer if you can't walk on the flats for extended bouts several times per week. Non-stop hill work is also very tough on the hamstrings and lower back.

I can only handle about an hour or so of treadmill walking at one time, but I know several marathon walkers who do their entire three- to five-hour long walks in the gym. Having the television or radio on will help to pass the time. If you plan on *buying* a treadmill, look for the following:

- A quiet, powerful motor—1.5 to 2.0 horsepower or more. Don't bother with non-motorized treadmills. Granted, they are much cheaper than motorized models, but you get what you pay for. It's almost impossible to get the belt moving on a non-motorized treadmill unless you're on a steep incline, and the belts often stick, causing you to stutter-step or trip.

113

- A sturdy deck that doesn't bounce across the floor when you walk on it.

- Variable speed, up to 8 miles per hour—or more if you do any faster running or racewalking as cross-training.

- Variable, electronically controlled elevation.

- A smooth belt at least four feet in length. The belt should also be padded so you don't feel the individual rollers that move it.

- Safety features like an automatic slow-start speed of 1 mph or so, front and side handrails, and an emergency stop button or "rip cord."

You're better off with a basic but sturdy treadmill without a lot of electronic gizmos than with a high-tech, but lightweight unit that bounces across the floor when you walk on it. One common feature of pricier treadmills is a built-in heart rate monitor. It's a nice touch, but you can buy your own portable monitor for a lot less than what the included monitor will add to the treadmill's cost. To get an idea which features you just can't live without, try out several treadmills at your local gym. Then be prepared to pay $1,000 and up (way up!) for a good new treadmill—but check the classifieds or a second-hand sporting goods store for great deals on used models.

Mall walking

Another option for many walkers is *mall walking*. Many indoor shopping malls open up early to allow walkers to get in their morning workouts. The most obvious benefit is the controlled environment. You're guaranteed ideal temperatures and dry conditions without the constraints of training on a treadmill. Water and bathrooms are also available during your workout, and there's bound to be a place to enjoy coffee or breakfast afterwards. Call or visit your local mall to see if they support a mall walking program. Some malls have organized clubs that offer members discounts at mall retailers and other perks. If your mall doesn't have a club, contact the National Organization of Mall Walkers at (573) 486-3945 to find out how to start a chapter in your area.

Water walking

Occasionally, an injury may keep me from my walking workouts for a few days or more. One of the ways I stay in shape is by walking in the deep end of a swimming pool. I get most of the benefits of walking on dry land, and the resistance of the water against my feet and legs really strengthens my walking muscles in a hurry—all with zero impact. Many health club pools will have a "wet vest" that you can wear to help keep you afloat, or you can use a styrofoam flotation belt. If the pool isn't deep enough to allow you to walk with your feet off the bottom, you can still get a pretty good workout by actually walking across the bottom of a shallow pool.

You have to do a lot of walking to train for a marathon. Where you walk is less important than the walking itself, but having enjoyable places to train will go a long way towards keeping you motivated. Wherever you choose to walk, don't feel "married" to one location. Variety in the kinds of workouts you do, and where you do them will make your walking more enjoyable. Just make sure anywhere you walk is a safe place to train, and make it even safer by training with friends and by wearing bright-colored clothes.

Steve Attaya on: Heading for the Hills

Age: 54
Marathon PR: 4:45:26
Marathons Completed: Mardi Gras '99, '00; Boston '00-'03; Blue Angel '01, '03; Mississippi '01, '02; Baton Rouge '01; Calif. Int'l '01; First Light '01, '02; Mercedes '02; Pike's Peak '02; Mid-South '02; Miss. Coast '02.

Steve, a sub-5:00-hour marathon racewalker from New Orleans, has been walking since 1998, and walking marathons since 1999. He began walking to lose weight—and lose weight he has! Once weighing in at 243 pounds, Steve cut down to 160 through a low-fat diet and a lot of walking, hiking, stationary-bike riding and even office building stair-climbing. Although the computer programmer admits he probably dropped the weight too fast—he suffered from gall stones after losing 50 lbs. in three months—Steve definitely prefers his current status as a marathoner and competitive racewalker to his past life as an avid couch potato and television remote control driver—as does Sara, his better half!

Steve's sub-sea level hometown of New Orleans is known for a lot of things, but elevation changes isn't one of them. So Steve trained for the Boston Marathon's legendary "Heartbreak Hill" by heading out to one of his "artificial" hill courses one or two days per week. Steve would walk up to fifteen miles on the ramps of five- and ten-story parking garages, or on highway ramps or bridges.

According to Steve: "Whenever I told somebody I was going to walk the Boston Marathon, the first words they would say were invariably, 'whoa, Heartbreak Hill!' so I knew I'd have to do some hill training to get ready. I really believe you need to subject your body to the kinds of conditions you'll experience in your races. It's easy to train for hot and humid races around here, but hills are another thing entirely. The biggest hill in New Orleans is a 24' pile of dirt in the Audubon Park Zoo, so I had to do a little searching, but I was able to find some good 'fake' hills. I used overpasses and bridges a lot, but my favorite hill-training course was the Loyola University parking garage. It has five floors, with good steady inclines up to each higher level. The ramps are shaded, but open enough to allow a breeze, and it's lit at night. I kept a pumpernickel bagel and fluids at the car and stopped every two to four laps. In the end, Heartbreak Hill was anti-climatic. My technique, muscles and mind were ready, and I'm certain the hill training made all the difference."

Chapter 18

Your Training Log

O nce you made the commitment to train for a marathon you undoubtedly tried to find as much information about walking the event as possible—this book included. You may even have a personal coach. But having great training information and a training schedule are only half the battle. Everybody has a different set of genes, different job and family situations, and different lifestyles, so everybody responds a little bit differently to their training. Consequently, two people following the same program can end up with very different results. The only way to learn what works best for *you* is to keep close track of your daily workouts. And that means keeping a training log or diary.

A training log allows you to learn from your successes and failures. When you have a good race, you can look back and see what you did right. If you have a less than stellar performance, you can find out what may have gone wrong. Your log can also be a great source of inspiration. Tracking your progress allows you to see how far you've come in your training, which can motivate you to do more and better training in the future.

You don't need an expensive walking-specific logbook to record your workouts. I use a hefty page-a-day daily planner, but all you really need is a simple notebook or calendar. Whatever you use, it should have enough room to include the following:

Morning resting heart rate

As you get fitter your stronger heart will be able to pump more blood with each beat. So your heart rate will be lower both at rest and at any given training or racing pace. Recording your heart rate every morning will help you to track your improving fitness. The lower it is, the fitter you are.

Heart rate can also be used as a very good gauge of overtraining. If your morning heart rate is more than 5 beats higher than normal you're probably fatigued and/or dehydrated and you should probably take a very easy day or even a day off.

Hours/quality of sleep

Changes in your sleep patterns can provide another early indicator of overtraining. If you have trouble falling asleep, or you wake up frequently during the night, you may be overtrained. Record the time you go to sleep and wake up, the number of hours you sleep, and the quality of that sleep. Take an easy day or two if you notice any major changes, or if you haven't been getting as much sleep as usual.

Body weight

Body weight can be used as an indicator of both hydration state and of overtraining. The difference between your weight before and after the workout can be used to show you how much water weight you've lost due to dehydration. (One quart of water weighs about 3 ½ pounds.)

If weight (fat) loss is a goal, weighing yourself in the morning instead of later in the day will minimize fluctuations caused by eating and drinking during the day. Aim for about one pound of fat loss per week. Losing more than that can leave you feeling weak and fatigued. If you aren't trying to lose weight, sudden weight loss can indicate overtraining.

Diet

You are what you eat. (Which means I'm a 155-pound box of Cap'n Crunch...) The food you eat is the fuel that gets you through your training walks and races, so your diet can profoundly affect your walking performance. Not enough carbohydrates and you won't have enough energy to get through your long walks. Too much simple sugar and you can get fatigued from an insulin induced "bonk." And not enough protein and you won't be able to repair your muscles after your workouts. These are the most common dietary "mistakes," but you may you have a very individual problem that affects your training and racing. Maybe you always have trouble getting through your long Sunday walk because you always eat a huge bucket of salty popcorn at the movies on Saturday night. Or maybe you get stomach problems after ingesting one brand of sports drink, but not another. Writing down everything you eat and drink can help you to solve these kinds of "training mysteries."

Weather

The weather can influence the quality of your training more than any other factor. If it's hot or humid your heart rate will be much higher at any given pace. With a higher heart rate you won't be able to walk as fast as you could on a cooler day. If possible, record the temperature and humidity at the beginning and end of your workout. The weather channel or an internet weather site can provide these values, or if you're a geek like me you can purchase a portable sling psychrometer for about $30 to take your own readings. A wet road can slow down your walking by adversely affecting your technique, while wind can help you or hurt you, depending on where it's coming from. Writing down information about all these variables can allow you to make better comparisons between workouts.

Scheduled workout

Your training log is a great place to write down your training schedule. It's right there at your fingertips, and you'll be able to compare what you did in training to what you intended to do when you read back over your workouts. If job or family responsibilities prevent you from committing to too much, just write out your key "must do" workouts for the coming week. Leave the rest of the days blank and just walk some easy mileage or cross-train on those less critical days.

Actual workout

Obviously, most of what you write down in your log will be the nuts and bolts of your workout: what you actually did, including details about your warm-up and cool-down, and mile, kilometer or even five-kilometer splits (intermediate times) for the workouts. You should also include heart rate values if you have a heart rate monitor. Be as specific as possible. Having this kind of detailed information will allow you to compare workouts over time to gauge your progress.

Perceptions

In addition to the objective details about the workout, you should also write down more subjective information like how it felt. It's okay to feel less than 100% from time to time, but if you feel like garbage for days or weeks at a time there's a problem—and more work probably isn't the answer. If I feel really good or really bad during a particular workout, I'll put a lot of detailed information about exactly what feels good or bad. But some days I'll just draw a little "happy face" (or sometimes a not so happy face!) instead of writing out the details.

Shoes worn

It's not a bad idea to write down which shoes you wear for your workouts. That way you'll be able to keep track of how many miles you put on them—anything over 500 and it's time to think about retiring them. You'll also be able to determine that a particular shoe may not be for you. If, for example, your knee hurts every time you wear your Nikes, but not when you wear your New Balances, it's probably a good idea to relegate the Swooshies to lawn mowing duty.

Cross-training

Finally, be sure to include information on your non-walking workouts. Swimming, weight-training, stretching, and other cross-training exercises are great for you, but they will have an impact on your walking. Keep close track on whether your supplemental activities are truly helping you, or just adding to your fatigue level.

With your personal history on paper you'll quickly learn what works for you and what doesn't. You're already an athlete. Keeping tabs on your training and learning what mix of hard work and rest is best for your body is a big step in becoming a successful *marathoner*.

EASY
25-30K at
The PARK

SUNDAY 28 MAY

30K

1 KMS	HR:	Avg HR	5 KMS:	
5:38³	134	(119)		↑-8:30 AM
5:36⁹	131	(131)		74° START
5:38⁷	133	(133)	28:19⁴	86° FINISH
5:45⁰	138	(135)		↑-90% HUM.
5:40⁵	140	(135)		
5:41²	137	(137)		
5:37⁷	138	(139)		Good one! 😊
5:38¹	138	(141)	28:10⁸	
5:35⁴	138	(134)		
5:38⁴	134	(138)		WORE NB 100ˢ
5:38²	142	(140)		Felt good.
5:37⁹	142	(142)	28:07	HOT and HUMID,
5:36²	142	(141)		BUT NO problems.
5:39⁹	138	(138)		HAMSTRINGS AOK!
5:40³	144	(138)		STOPPED for H₂O at 8k
5:38¹	145	(143)		POWER ADE AT 16+24k.
5:41¹	141	(142)		
5:33⁴	141	(140)	28:08	
5:34¹	141	(142)		
5:40⁰	142	(134)		
5:35⁸	145	(140)		
5:29³	144	(143)		
5:28⁶	140	(142)	27:40	
5:35⁶	142	(148)		
5:27⁷	146	(144)		Avg=5:33/KM
5:17⁸	154	(154)		
5:22⁴	164	(158)	26:32	
5:24²	157	(157)		
5:20²	157	(160)		
5:07⁶	168	(164)		

2:46:57

WEEK
TOTAL: 114 KM

SECTION III

THE RACE

Chapter 19

What to Wear

C ertainly the most important things you'll need to wear during your marathon are your shoes (Chapter 5). But what else will you need to keep yourself comfortable? That really depends on the conditions. The usually cool and dry Mayor's Midnight Sun Marathon in Anchorage, Alaska, and the notoriously hot and humid Honolulu Marathon will obviously demand different approaches.

Keeping cool

In terms of performance, keeping cool and comfortable is the single most important thing to consider when dressing for your event. So in a way, a race like the Honolulu Marathon is actually quite easy to dress for even though the environmental conditions are likely to be very tough. That's because there's not a whole lot you can do about the high heat and humidity except to wear as little as possible.

In a hot weather marathon you'll see walkers wearing anything from synthetic running shorts, to thigh-length tights ("bicycle shorts"), to casual walking shorts. Running shorts and tights are much less likely to cause chafing than casual walking shorts—trust me on that, you'll thank me later... On top, most male marathoners wear a racing singlet—a sleeveless mesh tank top. Many women like to wear singlets as well, as a top-layer over their JogBras, but some prefer to go with nothing on top but the JogBra. It's a matter of personal preference. Your shorts and top should be made from wicking fabrics like polypropyline or "CoolMax" that will pull moisture away from your skin to keep you dry and comfortable. Never wear cotton which retains 80% more moisture than synthetic fabrics. In any case, your clothing should be light-colored, and it's not a bad idea to wear a hat to shade your face and sunscreen on unprotected areas to prevent sunburn. Other than that, you're good to go.

125

A colder race is a lot trickier to dress for. You may be cold at the start, but after the first few minutes of walking you'll feel 10 to 20 degrees warmer so you'll have to make adjustments. And that means doing what your mom always told you to do: Dress in layers. The most important thing is to keep as dry as possible, so your first layer should be the same as what you would wear in a hot weather race: a singlet or short-sleeve shirt that wicks away moisture. The middle layer should be a warm insulating layer, perhaps a vest or shell made of a fabric that won't retain too much moisture or one that will keep you warm even when its wet. Wool or man-made materials like Gore-Tex or Polar Guard are excellent choices. The top layer should be light, breathable and waterproof, like a lightweight wind or rain jacket.

If it's cold enough to be uncomfortable at the start, but you're sure it will warm up, it's not a bad idea to go with a "disposable layer" or two. An old long-sleeve T-shirt or sweatshirt and a poncho, or even a large plastic garbage bag can be worn for warmth or to keep you dry while waiting at the starting line, and then discarded a few miles into the marathon. You'll be more comfortable without the extra layer, and as an added bonus most race directors collect these old clothes and donate them to the homeless. Just make sure you throw your extra clothes *off the course* so that other walkers behind you don't get tripped up in them.

If your top half is warm, you'll probably be pretty comfortable with only one or two layers on the bottom. If it's not horribly cold, your usual shorts should be fine; if it's below 45 degrees or so, you may decide to add a pair of tights or other non-restrictive leggings.

Identify yourself

Your race number needs to be visible at all times or you risk being pulled off the course as a "bandit"—someone who tries to race without paying the entry fee. Make sure the number is pinned to an item of clothing that you're certain you'll be wearing for the entire race. Most walkers pin the number to their shirt, but if there's a chance you'll be discarding your top shirt, you may wish to consider pinning your number to your shorts.

If you choose, your outermost layer of clothing can be more than a comfortable place to pin your race number. A lot of walkers write their names on their shirts so the crowds know who to cheer for. It may seem like a silly thing to do, but having thousands of people cheering your name all along the course is a sure-fire way to get yourself through any rough patches.

Socks

A good pair of socks is almost as important to a marathon walker as a good pair of shoes. Whereas shoes protect you from the roads, your socks protect you from your shoes. Without socks, your shoes can quickly turn your unprotected feet into bloody, blistered stumps. Your socks also protect your shoes from *you*. Socks will help to absorb excess sweat that can attract funguses, molds and bacteria that can reduce the life of your walking shoes—and cause nasty odors!

Choose your socks carefully. Cotton socks absorb and retain perspiration, and thick, wet socks can bunch up under your feet and toes and cause nasty blisters. Choose thin socks made of a wicking fabric like acrylic or CoolMax. "Thorlo" and "Double Layer" make excellent socks for marathon walkers. Cheapo tube socks are about the worst thing you can wear for a long walk—unless you like big, nasty blisters.

Make sure the socks you choose fit *your* feet. If you have narrow feet, a thicker sock will fill up space in your shoes, making them fit better. If you have wide feet, look for thinner socks. A really good pair of socks can run you $6 or more, but that's a small price to pay for blister-free feet and toes.

Fanny packs

If you plan on carrying anything with you when you walk, you may be able to get away with using a pocket in your shorts. Keys and money will fit in a small pocket, and now some manufacturers sell running shorts with a very big back pocket up by the waist band that's roomy enough for essentials like Power Gels, identification, money and a hotel or car key. But if your list of "essentials" runs to hat and gloves, Power Gels, sunglasses, medications, disposable camera, Vaseline to prevent chafing, Band-Aids in case of blisters, a few dollars for an emergency, a little toilet paper "just in case," etc., then you'll probably have to resort to a fanny pack. Try to find one that's big enough to carry everything you need, but not so big that it gets in the way of your walking. Fanny pack straps may cause chafing, so make sure you test yours out in training before deciding to wear one in a marathon.

Water carriers

Most marathons will provide plenty of water on the course, so you probably will not need to carry your own during the race. But training is another story. I do most of my training on loops so I stop for water every 8K (5 miles) or so. But for those long out-and-back courses you might want to consider buying a water bottle holder or other water-carrying device. Many manufacturers sell bottle holders that you wear like a fanny pack. One or two bottle versions are available, and most have extra pockets for car keys, money or Power Gels. "CamelBaks" are even more elaborate. A CamelBak is a cloth-covered plastic water pouch that you wear on your back like a back pack. A flexible plastic tube runs from the pouch to a Velcro stay on the shoulder strap. You drink from the tube just like a straw, leaving your hands free to swing as you walk. I use a CamelBak for long hikes, but I don't like the way it feels on my back when I'm racewalking. But I have seen a lot of people wearing them during marathons, so I guess it's a matter of personal preference.

Happy, comfortable walkers dressed for success out on the tank trail during the Mayor's Midnight Sun Marathon in Anchorage, Alaska.

A stopwatch

I highly recommend using a stopwatch, or *chronograph,* for training and racing. If your goal is to simply finish a marathon, then a stopwatch might not be critical. But it's possible that as you get stronger and faster with training you'll want to set a specific time goal for the race. A good watch that records "split" or intermediate times will "keep you honest" in your workouts, and will become even more important during the marathon itself. There will probably be clocks set up at every mile marker. That's great for the top runners, but if you started the race at the back of the pack and crossed the starting line several minutes after the actual start of the race, the time on the clock will be meaningless. But by hitting the split button on your watch at every mile marker you'll know exactly what pace you're walking without having to do any complex mental gymnastics.

I wear a Polar Coach heart rate monitor that records my mile splits along with my heart rate for every split. It also records my maximum and average heart rates, then downloads the data to my computer after the race and graphs the whole thing out. I think I can even program it to walk the dog, do the dishes and change the oil in my truck, but I haven't gotten to that part of the users' manual yet. I love the thing, but all you really need is a cheap stopwatch that will record at least 26 split times—one for each mile of the marathon. And you can get a watch that does that for less than 30 bucks at K-Mart.

The clock doesn't lie. If your training indicates that you can handle 12-minute miles in the marathon, but you find yourself hitting 10:30s, you'd better prepare to slow down or you'll end up hitting the wall later in the race. A stopwatch will give you that valuable race-saving information.

The Chip

Most of the bigger marathons require that you wear a "ChampionChip" laced to your shoe. The chip is a small, uniquely coded electronic tracking device that records your presence at various checkpoints throughout the race. The chip will record your exact finish time instantly, and many races will also track each athlete's progress live on the marathon web site so that friends and family can see how you're doing. Although some walkers buy their own chips for about $30, most marathons supply every racer with a rental chip free of charge. If at all possible, pick your chip up prior to your last pre-marathon workout so that you can tie it to your shoe to make sure it feels right.

Final warning

Whatever you decide to wear, you need to try everything out first in training—preferably during your long walks. These long walks should be dress rehearsals—literally. Your shoes, your socks, and every item of clothing, as well as sunscreens, sunglasses, fanny packs, etc., should be tested and re-tested many times in training before your marathon. Anything that chafes, blisters, irritates or doesn't wick sweat effectively needs to be replaced. Don't let a $2 pair of socks or a dazzling new pair of bargain-basement racing shorts keep you from your goal of finishing your marathon!

Great Walking Marathons:
Mayor's Midnight Sun, Anchorage, AK

If you like 'em wild and wooly, this one's for you! The Mayor's Midnight Sun Marathon in Anchorage, Alaska starts innocently enough in the parking lot of Bartlett High School, where walkers congregate before heading out for the first few miles on well-maintained paved roads and bike paths. Before long, though, walkers find themselves on an eight-mile stretch of a dirt and gravel military tank trail that runs through a pristine pine forest. Moose sightings are common and bear appearances—although less frequent—also occur.

Walkers start at 7 a.m., one hour before the runners, which allows for a generous nine-hour official cut-off time. The event is very popular with charity walkers, especially those from the Leukemia & Lymphoma Society, which features the race as one of its signature events. So much so that nearly three quarters of the race's 4,000 entrants wear Team in Training's distinctive purple singlets.

Porta-Pottys are scarce, but if you don't mind ducking into the bushes—and no one seems to mind!—there are plenty of quiet places to stop for a potty break. Once the course emerges from the woods you're back on a "real" road that takes you through mostly flat residential neighborhoods—keep an eye out for the stuffed musk ox in the upstairs window of one of the houses! The road gives way to another stretch of scenic bike trail that takes you through more woods, fields, and by duck-filled lakes. The final mile is a tough, but manageable uphill climb to the finish line at West High School.

The course may not be the easiest one to negotiate, and the crowds may be sparse, but the weather is almost always fabulous (partly cloudy with humidity averaging 40% and a temperature range between 55-70 F), and the event is extremely well organized. So if you can handle a few hills and some rough footing, and don't mind not having thousands of screaming fans cheering you on, the Mayor's Midnight Sun Marathon is one of the more interesting choices for first-time (or repeat) marathoners.

Chapter 20

Food & Drink

If you get nothing else out of this book, please remember this: Marathoning is all about energy conservation and fluid replacement. Your pace during the marathon should actually be pretty comfortable—about 1 to 2 minutes per mile slower than your 10K race pace. If you can keep from dehydrating, or "bonking" from carbohydrate depletion, you'll get through the race. If you can't, you won't. It's that simple. So eating and drinking the right things before and during the race are critical.

Practice makes perfect

Your liver, muscles and blood can only store about 2,400 calories of glycogen (carbohydrate). And since your brain relies entirely on glycogen as a fuel source, only 40% to 60% of that stored glycogen can be readily accessed by your working muscles. But you'll burn about *3,000* total calories during a marathon no matter what pace you walk, so to get through the race you'll need to burn a lot of fat to conserve those limited carbohydrate stores.

Long easy walks are what teach your working muscles to burn a higher percentage of fats so that your limited carbohydrate stores are conserved. Long walks and the proper post-workout diet also teach your muscles to store more carbohydrates between workouts. These are critical "skills" that will help you get through your marathon. But to get through those long training walks you'll need to be fully hydrated and "fueled up" before hitting the roads.

A high carbohydrate diet is critical. That doesn't mean colas and chocolate cake—although these are high-carbohydrate foods. A good marathon diet features lots of *complex carbohydrates*. Foods like fruits and vegetables, grains (including pasta and cereals) and starches like potatoes. You should strive to consume four grams of carbohydrate per pound of body weight per day during your marathon training. Read those food labels and do the math.

My motto is "a pizza a day makes the wall go away," but you'll have to find out what works best for you. If eating a high-carbohydrate diet is a drastic change from what you're accustomed to, make the change to your diet gradually. Try out any new foods before one of your easy workouts rather than before one of your critical walks, like an 18- or 20-miler. If all goes well, then try a similar meal before one of the longer walks, and if you can get through all of the long ones feeling good and with no gastrointestinal problems, then stick with that diet in the days leading up to your marathon.

Carbo-loading

You may have heard the term "carbo-loading" from some of your more experienced marathoning friends. Carbo-loading refers to loading your muscles up with glycogen before a marathon or long walk. Athletes used to carbo-load by first eating a very high protein diet for three days after their last hard pre-marathon workout. The high-pro diet deprives the muscles of carbohydrates. With the muscles starved of glycogen, the marathoner would then eat a very high carbohydrate diet for the last three or four days before the marathon. The high-protein/low-carb phase would shock the muscles into being super-receptive to glycogen during the high-carb phase. Or so the theory went. More recent research has shown that the muscles take in nearly as much glycogen during the high-carb phase *without* suffering through the high protein phase as they do with it, so most athletes skip the headaches, fatigue and grouchiness that are typical of the low-carb phase.

I recommend the "easy" method of carbo-loading—the high carbohydrate phase without the prior depletion phase. But I don't think this approach is much different from what you should be doing on an everyday basis throughout your training. You should *always* eat a high carbohydrate diet during your marathon training—at least 60% of calories should come from carbs. That percentage may rise beyond 70% in the last few days before the marathon, but don't overdo it! As always, try any changes in diet many times in training before settling on a pre-race routine.

Another important point: Carbo-loading doesn't mean carbo-bloating! The percentage of carbohydrates in your diet may rise a bit in

133

the week before the marathon, but total caloric intake should remain about the same—or even decrease a bit since you'll be cutting back on your training in the last few weeks before your race. Don't give yourself permission to pig out in the name of glycogen packing!

Where's the beef?

Some athletes misunderstand high-carbohydrate diets. High-carbohydrate doesn't mean *all* carbohydrate. In addition to the protein you need to build muscles, blood vessels, and red blood cells, about 5% of your metabolic energy comes from protein metabolism. So marathoners actually need more protein in their diets than weight lifters do, since we burn a lot more total calories than our iron pumping friends. Don't eliminate all protein in your diet when attempting to increase your glycogen stores.

Cheeseburgers are my favorite protein source, but there are plenty of less fattening choices like lean meats, fish and legumes. Whatever you settle on, remember: If it's not what you normally eat, phase in any changes gradually. Try any dietary changes many times in training first before making them a part of your pre-marathon meal.

Sports drinks, bars and gels

Using sports drinks like Gatorade, Powerade and PowerBar's Perform Plus is a very good way to supplement your carbohydrate stores while you walk. They can help you to breeze through your long walks and may well hold off "the wall" during your marathon. But again, try out sports drinks in training first—preferably before your shorter walks, then during your long walks. Some drinks may be too strong for your stomach to handle, causing cramping. And a drink with too high a sugar content will cause your stomach to draw water from your blood to help digest the sugar, which can cause dehydration. Diluting the drink with water can help prevent both of these problems.

PowerBar and other companies also make "energy" bars and gels that many marathoners rely on for an added carbohydrate boost during training and racing. They come in a variety of fat/carbohydrate/protein mixes, are quite portable, and some of them even taste pretty good! I've had great success with these products, but again, everybody is different, so try them in training first.

Sports drinks, bars and gels should be used either during, after, or several hours before training and racing. Never eat or drink anything with a very high sugar content within an hour or so of an important race or workout. The high sugar content can trigger a strong insulin response in some individuals, which can lead to a sudden drop in blood sugar. Blood sugar levels will bounce back to normal after a few hours, so it's okay to down a PowerBar or sports drink more than two hours before a race, but not within the last hour or so.

The body burns the extra sugar while exercising, so it's perfectly safe, and very beneficial to take in sugar *during* training or racing. Aim for about 250 calories of carbohydrates per hour. It's also a good idea to replenish carbohydrates as soon as possible after a long workout or race—within 15 minutes if at all possible. The sooner you get the carbs back into your system, the better your muscles are at storing them.

Whenever using energy bars and gels, keep in mind that your muscles store two grams of water along with every gram of carbohydrate, so be sure to drink plenty of water along with your "power fuels."

Even in Anchorage, it's never too cool to pass up the water tables.
Stay well hydrated: Drink early and often!

Water 'bout water?

Now, what about the world's oldest sports drink: water? Dehydration is far and away a marathoner's biggest enemy, and the number one reason people drop out of marathons. Dehydration can happen fairly quickly. *Hydration*, on the other hand, takes time, so it's something you need to keep on top of all the time. Those eight glasses a day your mom used to tell you about are just the beginning. To make sure I have my fill, I keep a 32-ounce bottle on hand at all times. I usually drink three or four bottles per day in addition to what I take in while I walk. Your intake should be about eight ounces every fifteen to twenty minutes of walking.

Although it's extremely unlikely, it is *possible* to drink *too much* water. A potentially dangerous condition known as *hyponatremia* can develop if you sweat a lot but only replace the water and not the minerals like sodium and potassium. Eight ounces of water every fifteen to twenty minutes of a 6 ½-hour marathon adds up to about 1½ gallons of water, which may very well be too much for some people. So make sure some of your fluid intake is in the form of sodium- and mineral-containing sports drinks. Drinking sports drinks, or even eating salty foods during your long walks and marathons is all it takes to prevent hyponatremia, so don't cut back on your water intake to prevent this very rare condition. Dehydration is much more common and much more dangerous. Drink up!

What about "dieting"?

If you're carrying a few extra pounds, dieting for weight loss— in combination with exercise, of course—isn't a bad idea. Any time, that is, except during marathon training. Cutting back on calories now will almost surely lead to carbohydrate-depletion and "bonking" during your long walks. Your immune system can also be adversely affected by dieting; and the last thing you need when training for a marathon is a cold or the flu.

If you are overweight, you should begin to lose body fat and inches as your weekly mileage increases. You will probably also lose some weight, but don't necessarily expect it. You'll be building muscle as you walk, and muscle weighs more than fat. Muscles also store a lot of extra water when they store glycogen, so your overall weight may not change very much even if you are losing fat. Lower body fat does equate to a higher VO$_2$ max, but you need your energy now. Don't pig out, but don't starve yourself either.

And vitamins?

Be *very* careful with these things. Back in 1991 and 1992 I was sponsored by an independent vitamin manufacturer. I began feeling really fatigued while training for the 1991 World Cup Trials so my vitamin guy suggested I take 200mg of this and 400mg of that. I got even worse, so he told me to take more supplements. I only got better when I forgot to take my bovine thyroid extract and my mega-whoopdeedoo heavy metal mineral pills with me to California for the trials race. A similar thing happened the following year in the weeks before the 1992 Olympic Trials, so I had some blood work done and discovered that my liver was so clogged up with fat-soluble vitamins, iron, zinc, magnesium and other metals that it had all but shut down.

Very few people are walking around these days with rickets or scurvy. Vitamin and mineral deficiencies are the exception not the rule, so avoid taking supplements unless you're sure there is a problem—and you're certain that vitamin or mineral supplements will cure rather than exacerbate the problem.

A daily multivitamin is probably safe for most people, and women may want to think about taking a daily with iron, but beyond that, get blood work done before trying to cure your real or imagined ailments with pills.

One last tidbit

Whatever you decide to eat or drink during your walks, practice, practice, practice! If you do discover any problems, keep a diet journal or take notes on everything you eat and drink in your training log to figure out what works for you. Your individual dietary needs, perspiration rate, gastric tolerance and emptying rates may be very different from mine or anybody else's.

Don't ever eat or drink anything during a marathon that you haven't tried over and over again in practice. The longer the race, the odder the stuff they'll try to give you along the course. During a 5K all you're likely to see are cups of water. In a 10K you may see Gatorade or some other sports drink. But in a marathon there's no end to what people will try to give you to keep you going. Beer, oranges and candy are common, and easily identifiable. But you may also be offered raw vegetable juices, "Green Magma," bee pollen or even weirder stuff. One of our Team in Training marathoners learned an important lesson the hard way during the Marine Corps Marathon. After enjoying oranges, candy, Power Gels and other goodies that volunteers and spectators handed him along the way, our friend was intrigued by a tasty looking gel the volunteers were handing out on tongue depressors. Only after sucking down a big wad of the stuff did he realize that the goop was actually Ben Gay. He still finished, but the experience left a bad taste in his mouth—literally!

Drinking and eating on the go are learned skills. Learn how to get as much water and carbohydrates into your body as you can well before your race by drinking lots of water and sports drinks, and possibly trying energy bars and gels during your long walks—a marathon is no place for on-the-job training!

Chapter 21

What to Expect on Race Day

If you've never walked a marathon before, you may be somewhat nervous in the days before the event. Fear comes from the unknown, so practicing a pre-race plan, and knowing a little bit about what you'll see before and during the race may help ease some of those jitters.

Pre-competition routine

There are a lot of important details that need to be taken care of before a marathon. Details like eating and drinking the right things, wearing the right shoes and clothes for the weather, and getting in a good pre-race warm-up. But you really shouldn't be wasting valuable "mental energy" debating what to eat, what to wear and how to warm-up right before the race. Your mind needs to be free to concentrate on the race itself, so these decisions should have been made long before the marathon.

The first rule of pre-marathon preparation, then, is to find a system that works for you and then use the same routine for all your long workouts, "test" races, and then for the marathon itself. By sticking to the same plan over and over again in training, your routine will be second nature come race day. So no matter how many distractions there are on marathon morning, you won't have to think about what to do to get yourself ready for the race when the time comes. And knowing exactly what you'll be doing before your big walk, and having practiced the same routine over and over in training will really help you to stay focused and relaxed.

Getting to Carnegie Hall

Practice makes perfect. Getting into your marathon "groove" is a lot like getting yourself ready for work every morning: You get up, feed the cat, eat your Fruit Loops, shower, dress and you're on your way. You've done it so many times before that you don't even think about any of these steps, you just get out of bed and do them. But it wasn't always that way. Perhaps for a while you tried eating a Sausage McMuffin in the car on the way to work, but those nasty grease stains in your lap put an end to that experiment. You've probably also tried different shampoos, tooth pastes, underwear and shoes, but for whatever reason, you've settled on the choices that make you the most comfortable.

And of course, the same goes for your pre-race routine. Try different meals, warm-up routines, shoes and clothes before your less important workouts until you find out what feels right every time. Then test the best of these routines before your long walks, and enter a few local races (5K to half-marathon) using the same routine beforehand to see how it holds up under real race conditions. If you're not comfortable with any part of the plan, try something else. Don't be afraid to make any adjustments to the pre-race warm-up that I—or any other coach or walker—have suggested. It's important to do whatever *you* need to do to feel good going into the marathon, whether it's "what everybody else does" or not.

Your pre-marathon preparations should begin well before race morning. You should have broken in your shoes and tried out your racing uniform many weeks before the race. Then a day or two before the marathon you'll pick up your race number and registration packet. The night before you should lay out all your clothes, shoes and things like Power Gels, Band-Aids and Vaseline to make sure you have everything you'll need during the race—just like your mother used to do for you before school. Pin your number to your singlet and make sure that everything fits properly—but since you've already worn everything at least a few times in training to test them out and break them in, they should be fine, right?

It seems any time I wait until race morning to get my gear together I always wind up with two left shoes, no racing shorts or not enough pins to attach my number to my shirt. If you're going to have something go wrong, let it happen the day before the race instead of the morning of, so you'll have time to solve the problem before race time.

You definitely want to be well rested heading into the race, so make sure you get to bed at a reasonable hour the night before. But don't turn in much earlier than usual because pre-event jitters may prevent you from falling asleep right away if you try to hit the hay too early. If the race is in a different time zone, or if you'll have to get up much earlier than usual to get to the start, go to bed a little earlier every night starting about a week before the race to reset your internal clock. Make sure you set the alarm (or two or three!) to get yourself up early enough on marathon morning so that you don't have to rush around like a maniac while preparing to go to the course.

Whether to eat or not the morning of the race is a matter of personal preference, but I think it's a good idea. You don't want to feel bloated, but you don't want to feel hungry either. I suggest eating a light (300 to 400 calories) meal at least two hours, but preferably four hours, before race time. If at all possible try to eat the same thing you ate before the best of your long pre-race walks, or what you ate before your previous best marathon it this isn't your first. Whatever you do, don't experiment! Do whatever has worked for you in the past.

Plan to arrive at the starting line at least 60 minutes before the scheduled start time to allow yourself plenty of time for a complete mental and physical warm-up—and to give yourself plenty of leeway in case there are traffic tie-ups, long lines at the Porta-Pottys or other unforeseen delays. In some of the bigger marathons you may even be *required* to check in at the starting area well before the start time— sometimes hours before. Don't let the waiting get to you. Bring a warm throw-away blanket, a snack, and newspaper to read and just relax until it's time to warm-up.

And speaking of warming up... A marathon doesn't require as much warm-up as a shorter race, since you'll have plenty of time to get the blood pumping by walking at an easy pace for the first few miles. Even so, you still want to make sure you're feeling nice and loose before the race starts. But one more time: No experimenting! Just do exactly the same warm-up that you did before all your long workouts.

One that works

Everybody is different. So you might come up with a pre-marathon warm-up routine that's different from anybody else's. But the routine I suggested in Chapter 13 seems to work for me and most of the people I coach. It always gets us to the starting line loose, warmed up, and ready to go:

- **Warm-up.** An easy 10- to 20-minute walk will help to work out the kinks and pump some blood into your muscles to facilitate drills and stretching.

- **Dynamic flexibility drills.** Perform five or ten minutes of drills from Chapter 11 to rev up your neuromuscular system and to extend the range of motion of your walking muscles. You don't have to do them all, just do the ones that help you to loosen up your chronically tight spots. And don't try any new drills before the race that you haven't done many times before in training.

- **Accelerations.** Three or four 40- to 50-meter accelerations will further enhance your range of motion. Start out walking at an easy pace with short, relatively quick strides, then build up speed. Be sure to get up to race speed to make sure your technique feels good at competition pace, then ease back down to a slow walk.

- **Stretch any "problem" areas.** If anything still feels tight or uncomfortable, spend a few more minutes *gently* stretching out these areas.

- **Go!** But don't go nuts. You're warmed up, loose, and full of adrenaline so it will be very easy for you to start out too quickly. Start the race at what feels like a very comfortable pace and you'll probably be right on. Go out too hard and you'll pay for it in the second half.

You may decide to modify the routine to suit your needs. It's okay, I won't be offended! But when you find a pre-race regimen that works for you, use it every time you race. And be sure to start your warm-up at least 20 minutes before race time. The last thing you want to do is show up at the starting line stressed-out, tight, and still tying your shoes and pinning your number on when the gun goes off because you didn't start your warm-up early enough. Not that anything like that has ever happened to me....

Pre-race logistics

Every race is different, but in any marathon there will be a starting line. If you happen to be a slower walker you don't want to start too close to the front or the runners will trample you when the race starts. Most marathons will have placards indicating where runners and walkers of various abilities should start. Bigger races even have "corrals" to separate participants into minutes-per-mile groups. Elite runners will start right at the starting line. 6-minutes-per-mile-pace runners will line up behind them. Then the 7-minute milers, the 8-minute milers and on down to the 18- and 20-minute pace areas.

It may take a few minutes to get across the starting line if you're at the back of the pack, but your chip will deduct those minutes from your finish time and by starting at the back you'll avoid feeling like a one-legged guy in a red shirt at Pamplona. If the race doesn't use the chip system, simply start your stopwatch whenever you cross the starting line. You *do* have a stopwatch, right?

You'll no doubt be at the race site long before the start of the race. If you've carbo-loaded and you've been staying hydrated, you'll almost certainly be looking for a restroom before the race starts. Even the smallest marathons will have plenty of Porta-Pottys near the race start, as well as several scattered every few miles along the course. They aren't the washrooms at the Ritz-Carlton, but they do the job. The problem with those Porta-Pottys though is that everybody else will have the exact same thing on their minds right before the race, so you may encounter some really long lines.

It's been my experience that there's *always* an alternative. At the inaugural Rock & Roll Marathon in 1998 there were rows and rows of Porta-Pottys, but the lines were 10 to 15 people deep. It didn't take long for me to discover that at the end of each long row there were a few extra sideways-facing *empty* johns that most of the other runners and walkers couldn't see from where they were standing! In urban marathons there will also be hotels, gas stations, diners, etc., within a block or two of the start. I've found that proprietors are always very accommodating on marathon day, so don't be afraid to take a quick walk around the block to see what else is available.

Once you've "taken care of business," complete your warm-up then line yourself up in the appropriate corral or pace section. A minute or two before the start, the race director will wish everyone luck and give any last-minute warnings or advice, then he or she will shoot the starting gun, cannon, or in some cases, fireworks, and off you go!

Expect the unexpected

When considering what to expect once the race starts, the best advice I can give is to be prepared for anything! Every race is different, so even the most experienced marathoners have to make adjustments during the race. Some races like New York and Chicago offer wild crowds and music to buoy your spirits from start to finish; others, like the Mayor's Midnight Sun, offer hours of solitude. Before taking a group of first-time marathon walkers to Anchorage in 1997 I told them how uplifting the cheering crowds would be. But once we set out on the course, we were greeted by all of two dozen spectators—and three or four of them were moose!

More important than spectators, is fluid replenishment. Most races will provide both water and sports drinks along the course. You should be able to get enough to drink without stopping if you know how to drink from a cup on the go. But again, expect the unexpected. I thought I had covered all the bases before the 1999 Mississippi Gulf Coast Marathon. I parked my car where the course map showed the 13-mile mark to be, and I stashed water bottles and Power Gels on the hood—just in case. As it turned out, the marathon's water sponsor provided tiny 6-ounce cups at the water tables. The cups were so small they were almost completely useless. When the time came I was really desperate for my 32-ounce water bottle, but I had read the map incorrectly, and the course veered off a few hundred yards before the spot where I left my car. I continued on, but was never able to make up the deficit. I bailed out utterly dehydrated at 20 miles. Lesson learned: If you can't get enough water on the go, STOP at the water tables and take as many cups as you need to keep yourself hydrated. Just make sure you look behind you before stopping suddenly or you may get rear-ended or inadvertently block another walker from getting her water.

I've had similar problems getting sports drinks in marathons. The Los Angles Marathon is generally one of the better-organized races on the calendar, but torrential rains during the March 2000 edition threw the volunteers for a loop. There was plenty of water. In fact the cups were overflowing, but sports drinks were few and far between.

With 23,000 runners and walkers competing for the same cups, I had a hard time grabbing cups of sports drink without stopping. In retrospect I should have stopped for a few seconds to make sure I got the carbs into me. By 19 miles I was very much on the verge of hitting the wall. Luckily, PowerBar came to the rescue with a Power Gel aide station. I downed three gels, which got me through to almost 24 miles, but I really struggled the last two miles. Same lesson as before: If you can't get enough to drink on the go, don't be afraid to stop. You'll get back those few seconds you lose by stopping when you don't hit the wall or become dehydrated in the later stages of the race.

Every race is a new and different adventure. Knowing *everything* that lies ahead would take away a lot of the fun of walking a marathon, but you should do everything you can to cover the important bases. Doing so is actually quite easy: All you need to do to walk a great marathon is to prepare specifically for the event you'll be walking (Chapter 22), stick to *your* plan, but then be flexible enough to roll with any of the unexpected challenges that inevitably crop up in any great adventure. If you do that, you can't help but have an amazing marathon experience!

Great Walking Marathons:
Walt Disney World Marathon, Orlando, FL

The Walt Disney World Marathon, first held in 1994, has in a few short years become one of the world's most popular "event" marathon destinations. It has everything you would expect from the architects of the Magic Kingdom: magical sights, sounds and surprises every step of the way. Mickey Mouse, dressed in the current year's theme costume, starts the race with the initial fusillade of a tremendous fireworks display, and you're off on an adventure that takes you through four of Disney's theme parks. Nearly all of the spectators are confined to the parks themselves, so Disney provides loads of entertainment on the roads between the different units of the Magic Kingdom, from costumed characters to bands and laser light shows.

The course is dead flat—total elevation change is only 30 feet—but lots of "Goofy" turns, tight spots, and in some years warm humid weather may prevent lightning fast times. But then again, fast times aren't necessarily the event's main attraction. Even so, there are inducements to finish fast: Every finisher receives a commemorative long-sleeve T-shirt, but only those coming in under seven hours receive the heavy Mickey Mouse finishers' medallions. (Half-marathon participants earn Donald Duck medallions.) And racewalkers may be eligible for even more goodies. For many years Disney character trophies and other awards have gone three-deep in 10-year age categories from 39 and under to 70 and over in the judged racewalk. Unfortunately, due to volunteer burn-out, the there was no judged racewalk in 2003, so its future is uncertain.

If you plan on bringing the kids to watch your marathon—or if you're a kid at heart yourself—Disney is sure to provide you with many magical marathon memories.

Chapter 22

Using Your Head to Finish Faster

A marathon is enough of a challenge without adding to the degree of difficulty by not using your head. Things like doing some pre-race reconnaissance, using the course to your advantage and pacing your way through the race can help make your marathon a little bit easier.

Reconnaissance

Knowledge is power. Reconnaissance means finding out as much as you can about your marathon well before the start. Good research should turn up obvious things like the exact location and time of the race start, but also details about the course, locations of aid stations and what kinds of drinks will be provided, as well as the likely weather conditions you will experience on race day.

Most marathons have web sites that contain all kinds of details about the race, including the name of the sports drink sponsor, an elevation profile and a printable course map. You should also receive an information packet by mail once you sign up for the race. Read everything you can about the race, and then take action. For example, make sure to buy some of the drink sponsor's product at least a month before the race so you can test it out in training. Look over the elevation profile so you know what you're getting yourself into in terms of hills. If there are a lot of hills, make sure you do at least some of your training on similar topography. If you live within a reasonable distance of the race course, do at least a few of your workouts on the course itself. If you don't live nearby, try to drive at least some of the course, if not the whole thing, the day before the marathon. If there are steep hills, get out and walk on them. Also take note of the turns, especially those at the beginning of the course when things are more crowded. You don't want to be caught on the wrong side of the road or you'll be forced to walk a lot farther going into the turn.

Finally, keep a close eye on the Weather Channel or an internet weather site so you'll know what kind of weather to prepare for. If it's likely to be hot, try to train during the warmest part of the day or wear an extra layer of clothing in training for the last 10 days to two weeks of training to acclimate yourself to the heat. If rain is in the forecast, be sure to pack the right clothes for wet conditions.

Using the course

You also need to use your head when it comes to using the course to your advantage. Walking *smarter* can improve your times as much as walking *harder* can. Everybody in the race will start at the same start line and finish at the same finish line. But not everyone will take exactly the same path between those points. Most walkers will follow the walkers ahead of them wherever they go, like lemmings to the sea. If there are cones marking the course, most walkers will follow the gently curving line of the cones—and over the course of a marathon they'll wind up walking up to a half mile farther than the smart walkers who *cut the tangents.*

Remember what our good friend Euclid said: The shortest distance between two points is a straight line. So stay alert. If the next turn in the race is a left and you're on the right-hand side of the road, you need to cut a straight-line path from where you are to that turn. If there's a water stop on the other side of the road, don't cut over at the last minute, plan ahead and start angling towards it as soon as you see it off in the distance. The shortened distances can really add up over the course of 26-mile race. Cutting the tangents is not "cheating"—race courses are measured along the tangents. If you *don't* cut the tangents you'll actually be walking *longer* than the certified race distance.

Hills are another feature of the course that can either help you or hammer you, depending on how you handle them. You need to walk aggressively going up hills, but you can't expect to maintain the same pace on a hill that you would on the flatter parts of the course. Instead, try to maintain a *constant effort* going up the incline so you don't send your heart rate skyrocketing. Since your stride length will be shortened on the way up the hill, you'll usually be able to maintain a relatively constant effort by simply walking with the same turnover rate that you were using before you hit the hill—even though your pace will be slowed somewhat by the shortened stride.

Whatever you do, stay relaxed and hold your form: Maintain your efficient, erect posture, bring your arms up just a little bit higher, and make sure you continue using that short, quick, efficient turnover rate all the way to the top and beyond the crest of the hill.

Whatever happens, relax. If your competitors push too hard on the way up the hill, let them go. They'll die by the time they reach the top, and you'll be able to catch them on the way down. If you haven't blown all your energy on the way up, it'll be a snap to walk fast on the down side. Take advantage of the free energy you'll get from gravity's pull; go fast, but concentrate on staying efficient.

The trick to downhill walking is *controlling* your pace. Since the hill will be falling away in front of you, you'll actually have to extend your lead leg out to the front a bit to keep yourself from spinning out of control. You should also hold your arms a bit lower than usual to keep your center of gravity down. Practice walking both up and down hills in training: Learning the proper technique before the marathon will keep you from overstressing or even hurting yourself during the race.

Racing strategies

There are a number of different ways to pace yourself through a marathon. You can go out hard and hang on as long as you can, you can try to maintain a steady pace throughout, or you can try to start out at a comfortable pace then go faster and faster from start to finish to *negative split*. Some strategies are better or "safer" than others, so make sure you put some thought into which one will work best for you. Then, as always, use your head! Don't get caught up in the excitement of the race and forget to stick to your race plan.

Blast off and burn out. This is the strategy of choice for the rank beginner; the guy in the black socks and Bermuda shorts who you see on television leading the New York Marathon for the first 400 meters. What they don't show are the pictures of the same guy gasping for breath, curled up in a fetal position next to a fire hydrant somewhere in Queens. The idea is to go out hard to break your competitors, then to

149

hang on as long as you can—hopefully all the way to the finish line. That usually only works if you're far superior to your competitors anyway, in which case you would have won no matter what strategy you used. If you like lactic acid, *rigor mortis*, and crashing into the wall, this is the strategy for you; if you like getting through your marathon comfortably, with a good overall finish time and without hitting the wall, don't even think about it.

Even in shorter races going out hard is a risky strategy—it's not always easy to judge how much is too much. But in a marathon you're almost guaranteed to crash and burn long before the end of the race and, if you finish at all, it'll be with a whole lot of difficulty and with a very slow time.

Steady pace. If you've done your long walks and marathon goal pace workouts, you should have a pretty good idea what pace you'll be able to handle for the marathon. The idea here is to start out at that speed and carry it through to the finish line. By walking a steady race you should be pretty comfortable most of the way, only feeling real fatigue in the final stages—if you've judged your starting pace correctly. It takes a little experience to gauge pace properly, but the rewards are great: a faster, easier marathon.

Focus is the key to maintaining your speed for 26 miles, especially in the second half of the race. As you get tired you'll probably begin to slow down without feeling it. Counting your strides every once in a while, and using a heart rate monitor will help you to maintain your speed, as will keeping a close eye on your times at the mile markers. If you're a first-time marathoner, you should aim for the same pace that you walked your 20-mile workouts—assuming you're racing in similar weather conditions. If you can make it to 20 miles in training, you should have little trouble holding that pace for 26.2 in the race.

Negative Split. Most marathon runs are won by "negative-splitting" athletes who take the pace out relatively conservatively in the early going, and then gradually accelerate all the way through the race, hitting their fastest miles at the very end. The same strategy works just as well for marathon walkers. Using a negative-splitting strategy will give your body a good chance to warm-up in the early going, allowing you to save the hardest walking for the end of the race.

150

To negative-split you should start out just a little bit conservatively, letting other walkers who start out too fast get away from you in the early miles. Then consciously accelerate by gradually increasing your cadence throughout the race. Since things will be getting tougher and tougher over the last few miles, and your stride rate may be decreasing from muscle tightness, you may not actually be picking the pace up very much, but you'll *feel* like you're going much faster at the end of the race. This strategy is very good psychologically since you'll be passing other walkers throughout the race. It can also help to keep you loose since you'll be working your muscles through a slightly different range of motion as you pick up the pace. Just don't start out *too* slowly. Your first few miles shouldn't be more than one minute per mile slower than your fastest miles.

Stick & Kick. Sticking and kicking—hanging on to another walker's pace throughout the race then blowing by them at the end—is a very "easy" strategy since the other walker does all the pacing work. It's a good way to take some of the stress out of racing, but the strategy does have its drawbacks. First, because you will have saved all your effort for that finishing kick, your time may not be as fast as it would have been if you had pushed the pace a little harder the whole way. And you can never be completely certain that you'll actually be able to out-kick your rival. Even if you're a stronger marathoner, the other walker might be able to walk faster than you over short distances—like that last 2/10 of a mile that you were looking forward to for 26 miles. Even worse, it's easy to get pulled along too quickly at the start of the race by a better walker, or one who may not have judged her early pace correctly. Doing so could cause you to hit the wall later in the race. Despite the drawbacks, if your primary goal is simply to beat a particular person, and you're confident that you have a faster finishing kick, sticking and kicking may be a good strategy for you.

Whichever strategy you choose, break the race down into sections and concentrate on one small segment at a time. I like to break the race down into three parts: the first 10 miles, the second 10 miles, and the last 10 kilometers (6.2 miles). Then I subdivide each of those blocks into manageable 5K segments. Walking a marathon is a bit like walking on a high wire: just focus on one step at a time and don't look down (or down the road, in the case of the marathon!) Keep your focus on one small block at a time and you'll be at the finish sipping champagne out of your walking shoe before you know it!

Chapter 23

The Start

The early miles of a marathon are all about **discipline.**
You've been training for months for this one milestone
event. You're tapered, rested, psyched up and ready to
go. And if your technique is good, you'll probably be able to walk for at
least a few miles at a pace that's two to three minutes per mile faster than
your intended marathon pace. Don't! It can be very easy to get caught up
in the excitement of the race and start out walking way too quickly. But
doing so can ruin any chance of a good race, and quite possibly keep you
from finishing at all.

If you start the race too fast your body will think you're doing a
hard tempo workout or a 10K race. Your muscles will think you need a
lot of energy to maintain that quick pace, but that you'll be stopping after
only an hour or two, so they'll turn on the glycolysis engine and burn up
your carbohydrate stores in nothing flat. If this happens you'll never
make it to the finish line.

Your starting pace isn't the only thing that can determine what
"fuel mix" your muscles will use. What you eat or drink in the early
miles can also have a big influence on whether you'll burn mostly
carbohydrates, or mostly fats during the rest of the race. If you start
drinking sports drinks instead of water too early your body will get the
message that your muscles should burn carbohydrates instead of fats
which could cause you to hit the wall later on. I try to take in a lot of
carbohydrates during a marathon, but I don't start until at least 90
minutes into the race. But even though you should avoid taking in sports
drinks in the first few miles, that doesn't mean you should pass up the
water tables. Drink early and often.

Your walking pace should feel very easy in the first ten miles of
the marathon. You will have done several 10- and 12-mile walks at the
same pace in training, so you know the pace. Don't push any faster!
Enjoy the easy feeling and just get those first ten miles under your belt.

153

Talk with other walkers (as long as *they* aren't pushing the pace too much!), enjoy the scenery, interact with the crowd, but make sure you're walking at your goal pace, or maybe even a few seconds per mile slower than goal pace.

I always subdivide the race beyond my broader 10/10/6.2-mile segments. Almost every marathon will have mile markers and clocks, and most of the bigger ones will have clocks every 5 kilometers as well. Use them. Take the race, and especially this first segment one 5K at a time—you don't want to think how much farther you have to go at this stage! Make sure those 5K splits are comparable to what you've done in training. An 8-hour marathon is about 56:53 per 5K or 18:18 per mile; a 6 ½-hour marathon is about 46:13 per 5K or 14:52 per mile; and a 5-hour marathon is about 35:33 per 5K or 11:27 per mile. Do the math (or refer to Appendix II) well before the race so you'll know what kind of 5K splits to expect.

After only three 5K marks you're already at 15K. With all the distractions and the excitement of the race, the first 15K will have gone by very quickly, but guess what? You're more than one third of the way to the finish! 15 kilometers is also nearly 10 miles—9.3 to be exact—so it's time to put this part of the race to bed and start thinking about moving on to the Middle Miles.

Great Walking Marathons:
Nokia Mardi Gras Marathon, New Orleans, LA

Like all New Orleans Track Club races, the Mardi Gras Marathon is a fabulous event for walkers of all abilities. Starting at the Superdome, the course meanders through the French Quarter on its way past Bayou St. John and City Park, then turns back to the Superdome where half-marathon participants get to stop to partake in jambalaya and "adult beverages." Marathoners continue on through the Garden District, on the way out to a loop under the towering oaks of Audubon Park, then back to the finish at the Superdome.

The course stays open for 6 ½ hours, but recreational walkers are offered an optional early start. Racewalkers in open, masters (40+) and grandmasters (50+) divisions compete for distinctive awards decorated with ceramic Mardi Gras masks.

Mardi Gras is a great race for fast times. The course has few turns, and is pancake flat except for one short and very manageable bridge that's crossed at miles 6 and 9. The smallish field of about 2,000 participants limits crowding and bottlenecks at water tables, and picture-perfect weather most years all contribute to the possibility of some very fast walking.

The race is uniquely New Orleans. I've walked a lot of marathons, but I don't ever recall being served at aid stations by burly, hairy male volunteers in red dresses, or by equally hairy drag queens in full Rocky Horror Picture Show regalia. I've also never had to work so hard to try to beat runners dressed as Holstein cows or wearing nothing but diapers. (I beat the cow, but the pacifier-sucking baby out-kicked me in the last mile…)

All marathons are exciting events, but few match the combination of perks that Mardi Gras has to offer walkers and racewalkers.

Chapter 24

The Middle Miles

The middle miles of a marathon are all about **maintaining focus.** You don't want to push too hard too early, but you also don't want to fall asleep and drop off your goal pace. There are bound to be a lot of distractions along the way—especially if you're walking in one of the bigger "event" races like New York, Honolulu, Disney or Rock & Roll. There will be bands, cheering crowds and lots of other walkers to talk to. Allow yourself to be distracted by them in the early miles, but at this point in the race it's time to concentrate on keeping yourself on your target pace. Don't get me wrong, enjoy the entertainment and the energy of the crowd, but don't let them keep you from your goal of walking a fast marathon (assuming that is your goal.)

Conversely, if you've chosen a smaller marathon, it'll be easy to fall off your pace in the middle miles without the excitement and energy of the crowd to keep you moving. Any way you cut it, it's important to maintain your focus in what can be the no-man's-land of the middle miles.

At the 10-mile mark you should assess how well you've been sticking to your race plan, and how good you're feeling. If all is well and you feel good, keep on pace. If you feel *really* good and you've done the training, it's probably even okay to pick up the pace a little bit. But don't be tempted to pick up the pace too much—there's still a long way to go. Get through these next ten miles before doing anything drastic—especially if it's your first marathon.

By the 10-mile mark you should begin taking in carbohydrate drinks. Don't stop taking water completely, but start alternating carbohydrate drinks with plain water at the drink tables. Your muscles will have already switched on to "fat burning" mode so the supplemental carbs will give you extra energy without causing any of the problems that may arise from taking in carbs too early in the race.

This is also a good time to head off any disasters like blisters or chaffing. If you do feel anything rubbing, apply some Vaseline to the area, or if have to, stop and take care of any blisters that may be forming. If you stop now for a few minutes you'll feel fine once you get moving again. But if you wait until the last few miles of the race to take care of these problems, you may be very stiff when you try to resume walking. Plus, those little problems will probably get much worse if you try to ignore them, so take care of them now before they become big problems, and while your legs are still feeling relatively fresh.

The same numbers game that got you through the early miles will make the trip to the twenty-mile mark go by much faster. The 20K (12.4 miles) mark is your next target, and right after that you'll hit the 13- and 13.1-mile markers. You're halfway there! That half-marathon mark is what really separates the glass-is-half-full people from the glass-is-half-empty people. If you want to get through this thing, take my word, it's half full! Think about how far you've gone and how good you still feel, rather than dwelling on how far you still have to go.

The way I look at it, by the half-way point I've gotten all those boring early miles out of the way and now I'm at the point where the fun miles start. The first half was just groundwork for the real part of the race that lies ahead. And the first major mile post of the second half of the race is 25K (15.5 miles). 25K is where I give myself permission to start picking up the pace a little if I feel like I can. It's almost 16 miles, which means there are "only" 10 miles to go.

After 16 miles I start working on one mile at a time until I get to that magic 2-0. There are only four miles between 16 and 20, which is nothing compared to the 26.2 miles of a marathon, but mentally, these can be tough ones to crack. Even if you stay right on pace, these are the miles that seem to take a little bit longer. You start looking for those mile markers a little bit farther out. Keep it together—once you get through these four miles, you've got the race in the bag! After 18 miles you'll hit the 30K mark at 18.6 miles—almost three quarters of the marathon is behind you and only 1.4 miles lie between you and the 20-mile mark!

If you've paced the race properly to this point you should get to 20 miles feeling tired, maybe a little stiff, but certainly not wrecked. You should feel excited that there are only 10 kilometers to go, rather than dreading what lies ahead. If you've done the training there's nothing to fear—the wall may lie ahead for those crazy runners who went out too hard, but not for you. You had the sense to walk, and the self-control to start out at your own pace.

But even if you did go out too fast and you hit the wall, you can still get through the race. Nobody cuts your legs off when you hit the wall. You just get really tired and have to slow down a bit. You may even have to stop for a few minutes to regroup, but you'll still make it to the finish.

Whether you've picked the perfect pace, or you've gone out a little too fast, at this point of the race think back to when you started your marathon training: Your long walks were probably more than six miles even in the earliest weeks of your training. You may have even done some 10K races along the way. And that's all you have to do now. With 20 miles behind you, all you have to do is keep on rolling for another 10K—6.2 miles—and you'll be at the finish line! Ahead of you lie cheering crowds, perhaps your friends and family, and people to hang a finisher's medal around your neck and take your commemorative race photograph. Right now you're a walker, but in 6.2 short miles you'll be a *marathoner!*

Chapter 25

The Wall

If you've spent any amount of time around other marathoners, you've probably heard them talk about "the wall." The wall is the point when your body can become depleted of carbohydrates—usually around 18 to 22 miles into the race. But elite marathoners rarely hit the wall. Top racers even accelerate over the final miles of a marathon without skipping a beat. Then why is it that recreational marathoners—especially runners—are always talking about this alleged wall? Well, because it *does* exist. Or at least it *can* exist—if you've improperly trained for, or paced yourself during, the race.

The wall can come almost anywhere you choose to put it. If you don't train properly, or if you start out too fast and burn off your carbohydrates early, you can "hit the wall" within the first ten miles of the race. Or if you train well and start your marathon at a conservative pace, you may never hit the wall. It's up to you.

Get over it, Fatty

Glycogen (carbohydrate) depletion is a debilitating condition that makes you feel like you're walking through a valley of Jello. But the good news is that glycogen depletion—and the wall itself—are preventable.

Your body can't create energy using *only* fat or *only* glycogen. At any pace it must use a combination of both. When you walk at relatively slow paces you burn a high percentage of fat, but you also burn some glycogen. When you walk or racewalk fast, you use up lots of glycogen, but also some fat.

Since even the thinnest athletes have enough fat in their bodies to get them through 26 miles of walking, glycogen is the limiting factor in getting through a marathon comfortably. Solid training and smart pacing are the keys to conserving glycogen and avoiding the wall.

"Longing" for the right workout

Proper training is your personal "wrecking ball" for flattening the wall. The bottom line is that 5K and 10K training does not prepare you for marathon racing, and can actually work against you in the longer race. By doing a lot of shorter, faster workouts, you prepare your body to burn carbohydrates efficiently (aerobically) so that you don't cripple yourself with lactic acid during your 5K and 10K races. The key is mixing a lot of oxygen with a lot of carbohydrates within your muscles to produce a lot of energy. You do train yourself to walk a lot faster by doing a lot of short, fast workouts, but you also wind up burning a lot of carbohydrates in the process. That's fine for a race lasting 20 to 90 minutes, but carbohydrate depletion is Public Enemy Number One to marathoners.

Long, easy workouts are the key to successful marathon training. So the good news is that you get to slow down the pace of your workouts. The bad news is that you have to really up your mileage— especially the mileage of your long day.

Long easy walks teach your muscles to preferentially burn fat as a fuel. And since fat is—shall we say—"bountiful" in most of our bodies, this is obviously a good thing. The more fat you burn, the more glycogen you'll have to get you through to the Budweiser "refueling station" at the finish.

Don't be a knucklehead

Even if you train the right way, you can still goof up if you really want to. Once the race starts, you can influence whether your muscles burn mostly glycogen or mostly fat by how you pace the first few miles. If you start out like a maniac when the gun goes off, your muscles will think you're racing a 5K and they'll use up most of your limited glycogen supply within the first 90 minutes to two hours of the race. Then when you hit 30 to 35 kilometers (18.6 to 21.7 miles), you'll be so glycogen depleted that you won't even be able to burn fat efficiently anymore, which will leave you with just about nothing to fuel your final miles. If, on the other hand, you tuck this page into your shorts and re-read it just before the gun goes off, you just may be able to act appropriately and save your race. By starting off at a conservative pace you'll "tune" your muscles to burn a high percentage of fat throughout the race, thus sparing glycogen. Doing so will ensure that you have enough of both fuels—fat and glycogen—to get you through the race comfortable, and allow you to fly through the final miles like the elite racers do. If you get out the door and do those endurance-building long days, and you don't sprint away from the starting line like a scared rabbit, then you'll have plenty of energy to get you to the finish. So now you have no excuses for crawling through the last 10K of your next marathon: Get out and train, use your brain, or else the wall will remain.

And what if it does?

Hypothetically, let's say you *didn't* gauge your starting pace perfectly or you didn't get in enough long walks. What if you *do* hit the wall? Well, you're going to feel tired. Very tired. But you can still get to the finish line if you want to—and I don't mean in a taxicab! If you're willing to take it slowly, you *can* keep yourself moving towards the finish. You can pretty much forget about a blazing finishing time if you hit the wall, so just take care of yourself. Drink plenty of whatever sports drink it is they have at the aid stations, stretch as often as you need to, and take it one mile at a time and you'll get through it. It's even okay to sit down and take a five-minute break if you feel you can't go on—especially if you do it near an aid station so you can fill up on Power Gels, sports drinks and water. After a few minutes of rest and a good sugar "rush" you'll be amazed at how much better you'll feel.

Even with the sugar boost, you'll probably still be very tired, and the last few miles will still be pretty tough. It's perfectly normal to feel a little down in the dumps after hitting the wall. Don't sweat it. If you go through a bad patch, use the other marathoners around you for motivation. Unless you're the lead dog, there will always be people ahead of you to focus on, track down, and pass during the race—especially in the closing miles. Use them. Look ahead a few dozen meters to a good target: the guy in the girlie pink shorts, that goofy looking runner way up there, or the juggler in the gorilla costume. Don't pick someone who is clearly dying—even if you're having a hard time yourself, you're going to catch him anyway. Pick someone who looks strong, but who's not pulling away from you. Use their strength to keep yourself going. When you catch your target, urge them to work with you. If they can't keep up with you, drop 'em like sack of hot potatoes.

All those people around you, the guy in the gorilla costume, the guy in the pink shorts, and sure, maybe even that goofy runner, they're all human and they're all hurting. And most will fold like a napkin when the going gets tough. A few will be tough enough to fight through it and keep giving it their all. Make sure you're one of the later.

You've put a lot of time and effort into training for your marathon. The only reason you should ever drop out before the finish line is if you end up with a painful injury that's bad enough to cause a limp, or if you have suffered some other fairly major medical emergency. (And no, feeling really tired is not an emergency!)

According to Tim Noakes, a world-renowned exercise physiologist and MD, there are only three reasons you should ever consider quitting a marathon:

- **Severe vomiting or persistent diarrhea.** Both may indicate that something is seriously wrong. In addition to being just plain unpleasant, they both cause sudden loss of body fluids and electrolytes that must be replaced. If you do decide to carry on, drink plenty of water, but make sure you replace the electrolytes as well with some sort of sports drink or you put yourself at risk of developing hyponatremia ("water intoxication").

- **Light-headedness, drowsiness or aggressiveness.** These symptoms may be signs of hypoglycemia, hyperthermia (excessive body heat) or hypothermia (loss of body heat). Immediate ingestion of carbohydrates should reverse a case of hypoglycemia. If you don't respond to the carbs within 15 minutes, you may be hyper- or hypothermic and you should stop to cool yourself down, or warm yourself up, depending on whether you're overheating or suffering from "the chills."

- **Chest or stomach pain.** If the pain is just a side "stitch" it should go away almost immediately after you stop walking. If it doesn't stop, especially after you sit or lie down, it could indicate an impending heart attack, in which case you will obviously require <u>immediate</u> medical attention. Heart attacks during marathons are extremely rare, but it's better to be safe than sorry—or dead. Find a spectator or race volunteer with a cell phone and call for medical help immediately.

Even if you don't suffer any of these unlikely, but serious medical conditions, hitting the wall is no picnic. But it isn't enough to keep a strong-willed person (like you!) from getting to the finish line. In most cases you'll just feel very, very tired after hitting the wall. (Although sometimes extreme fatigue can actually be sort of fun... Hallucinations and wild food fantasies are surprisingly common, so don't be surprised when the person you've been chasing turns into a giant strawberry or a slice of cheesecake.) If you have to, slow down a bit, but try to keep moving towards the finish. Drink plenty of water, and eat or drink something with a lot of carbohydrates in it to get yourself through the rough patches. Again, it's even okay to stop and rest for a few minutes. Do whatever it takes to get over that wall, then keep moving towards the finish. Getting through 18 or 20 or 22 miles is certainly impressive, but you're not a marathoner until you make it through the whole 26.2!

Judi Allen on: Surviving the Wall

Age: 57
Marathon PR: 6:46:30
Marathons Completed: Bermuda '98, Rock & Roll '98, Disney '01, First Light '01.

Judi, a 14-year breast cancer survivor, knows a thing or two about surviving the wall as well. I first met Judi at one of my World Class walking clinics where she let us know that she trained a steady 3.1 miles per week—since the only walking she did was in the local 5K races. So it was a big step for her to sign up with Team in Training to walk the 1998 Bermuda Marathon. Judi has really excellent racewalking technique, so she felt great at the start of the race. After a few easy miles with the rest of the team she took off like a shot with one of our strongest walkers. We tried to convince her to take it easy for the first half, but her competitive juices and the excitement of the race got the better of her. Predictably, poor Judi hit the wall—hard.

Judi says: "In Bermuda I started out walking with another member of the team and found out too late that she had run a marathon before and considered herself more of a runner than a walker. As we walked and talked we started getting faster and left the rest of the team in the dust, against the advice of my coaches. The other team member finally ran off and left me and I started slowing down. Eventually other team members started catching up with me and passing me. Finally, as I started up a big hill at 16 miles I hit the wall. I think the worst part of it was when I finally stopped to sit on a curb to take a break, I looked up and saw that I was sitting right across from a cemetery!

"My coach got me moving again with lots of water, PowerBars, and M&Ms. I had to slow down a lot to finish, but as long as I kept finding reasons to laugh, and kept telling myself to keep moving in the right direction—towards the finish line and away from that cemetery!—I knew I would make it. After the race I realized what I did wrong so I went to the Rock & Roll Marathon in San Diego six months later to redeem myself. In San Diego I started out a lot slower—maybe even a little bit too slowly. But even with a bit of a knee injury, and 18 minutes of waiting for Porta-Pottys along the way, I wound up feeling great all the way to the end and finished the race faster than I had in Bermuda."

Chapter 26

The Finish

The last few miles of a marathon are all about **giving it your all.** Assuming you've judged your race properly, you should be able to maintain your pace or even pick it up a little bit over the last ten kilometers (6.2 miles). Chances are you'll be tired, but you'll find that the closer you get to the finish, the easier it will be to keep yourself moving.

This is the stage of the race where your conservative pace from early on is rewarded. You'll be passing all kinds of people who started out too fast—both walkers and runners. In fact, you'll be amazed how many recreational runners wind up walking 20-minute miles at the end of the marathon after hitting the wall.

At this point "all it takes is all you've got." There's no reason to hold back. You don't want to start sprinting with six miles to go, but you should start a gradual acceleration at this point—if you have the energy to do so. Your body will tell you how much you can push. If your breathing becomes labored, back off a bit. If you're tired, but you can still accelerate, up the ante a little bit with each passing mile.

This late in the game you'll definitely be taking things one mile at a time, but those 5K markers can still come in handy to further sub-divide the remaining miles. After 21 miles start looking for the 35K mark at 21.7 miles. Once you hit 35K it's only three tenths of a mile to the 22-mile mark, and from there only 4.2 miles to the finish! Looking for those mile posts may not seem important now, but after 20+ miles of walking these little psychological games may be all you have to keep you moving towards the finish line.

Keep giving it your all. At 23 miles you have just over 5K to go. Think back to your months of training: Remember all those "EZ 30-45 min" workouts? They were the easiest workouts of the week, but that's all you have to do now to finish! If you happen to be walking your marathon for a charity, think about your patient honorees. They've gotten through a lot worse than you've endured today, haven't they? Finally, think about the finish line. It's not just the end of the marathon, it's the beginning of your life as a marathoner. All you have to do now is get yourself through one more quick 5K and your spouse and co-workers will be lavishing you with praise and gifts for weeks!

The last three miles are both the hardest and the easiest miles of the race. You will be tired, but there are so very few steps remaining anyone can do it! It takes a lot of guts to get through the first few miles of the race when you know you have more than 20 miles between you and your goal, but right now, how tough do you have to be to walk a measly three miles? Just keep plugging away and you'll be at 26 before you know it. Then it's just two tenths of a mile to go! If there's anything left in the tank, gun it. But make sure you have a smile on your face when you cross the line because the cameras will be waiting for you!

After the race

After you cross the finish line and have your finisher's medal hung around your neck, walk around slowly to gradually bring your heart rate down. Don't sit down. If you don't keep moving, your muscles will stiffen up and you'll feel much worse once you try to get up again. Try to drink as much as possible—preferably sports drinks to replenish carbohydrates, but water is also fine if it's all you can find. If your stomach can handle it, it's also a good idea to try to eat some fruit or a carbohydrate-rich sports bar as soon as you can. Your muscles are most receptive to carbohydrates within the first two hours of the race. A little protein will help your muscles to store even more glycogen and it will also help to repair damaged muscles.

Your body has a way of letting your mind know exactly what needs replenishing, so don't be surprised by any weird cravings you may have. Mine tend to range from Taco Bell Gorditas to pineapple and ham pizzas, but don't let my cravings influence what *your* body wants after the marathon. And whatever you crave, no matter how weird, cave into it! Give yourself permission to indulge.

You may be tempted to soak in a hot tub or Jacuzzi after that double bacon cheeseburger, but you really shouldn't. You don't necessarily need to subject yourself to a cold shower after the race, but try to avoid very hot water. Heat will dilate your blood vessels, causing swelling in your sore muscles. If you're staying somewhere with a

166

swimming pool, standing in the cool pool water at least up to your hips will reduce swelling and does wonders for your tired feet and legs. Taking an anti-inflammatory like Advil is another way to help keep the swelling down. After getting out of the pool or shower, take a short—or not so short—nap. Then get up and take an easy walk, and keep drinking water to keep from tightening up too much—you'll need to get those legs working again if you want to dance at the post-race victory party!

Keep a bottle of water with you and continue hydrating the rest of the day and night. If you do attend a victory party—and most marathons have one—it's okay to have a few "adult beverages." But continue drinking water—at least one glass of water or sports drink for every "other" beverage you consume. When the evening winds down, unplug the alarm clock, take the phone off the hook, draw the shades tight, and tuck yourself in for a nice long rest. Try to sleep in as late as you can. If you do get up to use the bathroom, take another drink before going back to bed. You've had a long day, so you'll need a long night of sleep (or two or three...) to start healing your tired muscles. Repeat after me: One sheep, two sheep, three shzzzzz...

Chapter 26.2

"The Morning After"

Maybe you shouldn't read this chapter until *after* the race, because what I'm about to say may not be the best motivation to walk a marathon: You're probably not going to feel all that great for the first few days after the race. Your feet will probably hurt, you'll have some sore muscles, and you'll probably be pretty tired. Your immune system will probably be compromised, so if you try to do too much and don't give yourself enough rest, you may wind up catching a cold. In fact, you may well have a full-blown "marathon hangover."

The good news is that it probably isn't going to be a whole lot worse than anything you felt after your longest training walks, and most of those aches and pains will go away after a few days of rest. But that can be a double-edged sword. You may feel so good after the race that you'll want to jump right back into heavy training. Or you may decide to jump right back into racing shorter races—why let all that hard training go to waste, right? Wrong! You may feel great, but your muscles and joints will be weakened from the hard effort.

Take it very easy for the first two weeks after the race— especially if it was your first marathon. Sure, you can get out and walk a few easy miles every day, but don't do anything too long or too fast. I've never sustained an injury in a marathon. But I have wound up with more than a few in the first week or two *after* the race because I didn't respect the distance. Sometimes I felt so good after the race that I jumped right back into training and wound up paying the price. Do what I say, not what I do!

Take care of yourself

You'll recover more quickly from your marathon if you continue doing the same good things that helped you to get through your marathon training:

- Continue drinking water.

- Maintain a high-carbohydrate diet for at least three to five days after the marathon to fully re-load your muscles with glycogen.

- Gently stretch your muscles to help them regain their range of motion.

- Spring for a professional massage to speed healing of overused muscles.

- Consider taking "safe" supplements like Vitamin C and echinacea to help boost your immune system.

Looking down the road

After a few weeks you'll probably start to miss your training walks. You'll miss the camaraderie of walking with your training buddies, or the solitude of your long walks alone. At this point it's probably safe to get back into training, either for shorter races, or if you still have the bug, for another marathon.

If you do decide that you're up for another challenge, get out a calendar to start plotting your next marathon. Then follow the same rules that got you to the finish line of your last marathon. You won't have to start from scratch—your last long day, after all, was 26.2 miles! And with all the valuable experience you've gained—and all those miles under your belt—your next marathon is sure to be a personal record! Just make sure you don't overdo it. If the marathon you just completed was your first, give yourself a full six months before doing another. With more experience you can safely walk a marathon once every three months or so, but doing too many in a row can easily cause "burnout" or injury.

Of course it's also quite possible that your goal was to do *a* marathon—singular. That's okay, too. Most people who climb Mt. Everest only do it once. Really, what do you have to prove? You've done it—you're a marathoner. And you're a stronger person for it. So it's possible that you'll decide to put marathoning behind you and move on to new and different challenges. But no matter what you choose to do from here, there's no doubt you can do it. Because once you've walked a marathon, anything else you choose to do in life will seem more manageable. Many months ago you had a seemingly impossible goal: to finish a 26.2-mile marathon. Now you've done it. And now, marathoner, you can do *anything!*

There's nothing to whine about... it's *only* a marathon!

SECTION IV

APPENDICES

Walker-Friendly Marathons

Many marathons permit walkers to enter—meaning they'll gladly accept your entry fee money. But few marathon directors really go out of their way to accommodate walkers and racewalkers. The following are marathons that do. These races feature things like special racewalking categories and prizes; an early start or longer cut-off times for slower walkers; finish lines that stay open until everyone is off the course; and special clinics for walkers at the pre-race expo. These events have traditionally been good to walkers, but be sure to call or visit race web-sites for current policies. Also, don't assume a marathon is not walker-friendly if it is not on this list. I've only listed marathons with over 500 entries because these are the events that walkers are most likely to travel to. But more and more race directors are opening up to the idea of having walkers in their races so you may be permitted to enter your local marathon as a walker—again, contact the race director for details.

Best marathons for racewalkers

BAA Boston Marathon
Date/field size: April/15,000 runners, 15-20 invited racewalkers
Racewalk awards: Exhibition event, no awards. Entry by invitation only for sub-5-hour racewalkers. Contact Justin Kuo at kuo@world.std.com for info.
Time limit: Timing stops after 6 hours.
Why do it? Because it's Boston! Far and away the world's most prestigious marathon; 1.5 million spectators; a 100+ year history.
Web Site: www.bostonmarathon.org
Phone: (617) 236-1652

City of Los Angeles Marathon

Date/field size: March/23,000 runners, 200 racewalkers

Racewalk Awards: Yes. Age-group award winners receive plaques and merchandise awards (watches, cell phones, etc.)

Time limit: No time limit, but streets re-open after 6 hours.

Why do it? Over 1 million spectators; 115 live bands and performers line the course. Well-manned water/aid stops every mile. It's pretty hilly, and a little crowded, but definitely a fun event.

Other Events: 5K, and "Senior Walk."

Web Site: www.lamarathon.com

Phone: (310) 444-5544

Detroit Free Press/Flagstar Bank Marathon

Date/field size: October/4,000 runners, About 70 racewalkers

Racewalk Awards: Yes. Awards to top six male and female racewalkers.

Time limit: 5:45. Walkers start 15 minutes before the runners.

Why do it? Racewalk awards, of course, but it's also an "interesting" race. The marathon starts at Tiger Stadium in Detroit, then goes over the Ambassador Bridge into Windsor, Ontario Canada, along the Detroit River waterfront to the Windsor-Detroit Tunnel under the Detroit River to Belle Isle, then back to Detroit for the finish in Tiger Stadium. A flat course and cool weather are good for fast times. Entrants must apply early so that customs and immigration inspectors can review the applications.

Other Events: 10K, 5K Fun Run/Walk.

Web Site: No web site, but there is information at www.runmichigan.com

Phone: (313) 259-7749

Duke City Marathon (Albuquerque, NM)

Date/field size: September/5,000 runners, 50 racewalkers

Racewalk Awards: Yes, open and masters divisions in the marathon, half-marathon and 5K. Some years there are cash prizes for walkers.

Time limit: 7 hours

Why do it? Flat course, but the altitude will adversely affect your finish time.

Other Events: Half-Marathon, Marathon Relay, 5K, Kids' Mile, Senior "K" (one kilometer).

Web Site: www.dukecitymarathon.com

Phone: (505) 890-1018

First Light Marathon (Mobile, AL)

Date/field size: December/1,000 with about 25 racewalkers

Racewalk Awards: Yes. Five-deep awards for overall men and women.

174

Time limit: 8 hours.

Why do it? Race director is very willing to cater to walkers and racewalkers. Great weather, beautiful course, party at Dave & Mo's house afterwards! Awards hand-made by residents of a local home for mentally-challenged adults.

Other Events: Half-Marathon and 3K also award racewalk prizes.

Web Site: www.firstlightmarathon.com

Phone: (251) 476-8732

Honolulu Marathon

Date/field size: December/33,000, Several thousand walkers, about 50 racewalkers.

Racewalk Awards: Yes. Plaques to the top 3 overall male and female racewalkers.

Time limit: No time limit.

Why do it? No brainer: it's Honolulu in December. The racewalk awards and cowry shell lei finishers' medals are a big plus, but the heat, humidity, hills and huge field make PRs hard to come by.

Other Events: 10K Mayor's Walk.

Web Site: www.honolulumarathon.org

Phone: (808) 734-7200

New Jersey Shore Marathon (Sandy Hook to Long Branch, NJ)

Date/field size: April/1,100

Racewalk Awards: Yes. Awards to the top three overall male and female racewalkers.

Time limit: 7 hours

Why do it? The cool lighthouse awards; shoreline views and the stadium finish.

Other Events: 15K Fitness Walk.

Web Site: www.mcmarathon.org/MCMHomepage.html

Phone: (732) 578-1771

Johannesburg (South Africa) Big Walk

Date/field size: August/3,800

Racewalk Awards: Yes, including prize money. Medals to the top 3 in five age categories for males and females.

Time limit: None

Why do it? Big walker-only event, with marathon, half-marathon and 8K races.

Other Events: Half-Marathon and 8K.

Web Site: None

Phone: 011-802-1696

Lake Tahoe (California) Marathon
Date/field size: October/1,000
Racewalk Awards: Yes
Time limit: 8 hours
Why do it? Racewalk awards, beautiful course. Before/after there are casinos, restaurants and a variety of outdoor activities.
Other Events: Half-marathon, 10K and 5K racewalks have awards for walkers.
Web Site: www.laketahoemarathon.com
Phone: (916) 544-7095

Las Vegas (Nevada) International Marathon
Date/field size: February/1,500 in full marathon
Racewalk Awards: Yes, but only in the half-marathon.
Time limit: No, but traffic control stops at 5 hours.
Why do it? Most racewalkers choose to enter the half-marathon, but the 600 ft. elevation drop in the marathon almost ensures record times.
Other Events: 5K, Half Marathon, and Regional Half-Marathon Racewalk Championship.
Web Site: www.lvmarathon.com
Phone: (702) 876-3870

Nokia Sugar Bowl Mardi Gras Marathon (New Orleans, LA)
Date/field size: Early February/3,000 runners & walkers, 40 racewalkers
Racewalk Awards: Yes. 3-deep for men and women.
Time limit: 6 ½ hours, but slower walkers permitted to start early.
Why do it? It's a great way to tour the ultimate party town; racewalk awards are ceramic Mardi Gras mask plaques; jambalaya and adult beverages at the finish in the Superdome.
Other Events: 5K and Half-Marathon, which have 3-deep racewalk awards in Open, Masters (40+) and Grandmasters (50+) divisions.
Web Site: www.runnotc.org
Phone: (504) 482-6682

Portland (Oregon) Marathon
Date/field size: Early October/5,000 runners, 1,500 fitness walkers, several dozen racewalkers
Racewalk Awards: Yes. Awards to top 3 open and masters men and women.
Time limit: 8 hours
Why do it? Portland has long been known as THE walker-friendly marathon.
Other Events: 10K Walk.
Web Site: www.portlandmarathon.org
Phone: (503) 226-1111

San Diego Marathon
Date/field size: January/2,200
Racewalk Awards: Yes.
Time limit: No time limit, but course opens to traffic after 5.5 hours.
Why do it? Racewalk awards, although the race is reportedly not rigorously judged.
Other Events: Marathon Relay, Half-Marathon, 5K, Kids Mile.
Web Site: www.sdmarathon.com
Phone: (888) 792-2900

USATF National 40K Racewalk Championship (Ft. Monmouth, NJ)
Date/field size: September/Approx. 50 racewalkers
Racewalk Awards: Yes. Open and age-group awards. There are usually cash prizes for top walkers.
Time limit: None
Why do it? For anyone interested in a "real" long-distance racewalk—no runners allowed—a good bet would be the 40K National Racewalk Championship held each September, on the grounds of Fort Monmouth, New Jersey. The race is staged over a flat fast course at the Army post under the auspices of the Shore Athletic Club. The 40K distance (24.8 miles) is just a tad short of a full marathon. (The marathon is not a standard racewalking distance—only 20K and 50K events are held in the Olympics.) Best of all, there are no huge crowds to cope with, and no runners in gorilla suits to steal *your* spotlight. The race is directed by Elliott Denman, a 1956 USA 50K walk Olympian who has raced 20 consecutive New York City Marathons.
Other Events: 20K Racewalk.
Web Site/E-mail None/Elliottden@aol.com
Phone: (732) 222-9080

Best marathons for slower walkers
Air Force Marathon (Dayton, OH)
Date/field size: September/3,000
Racewalk Awards: No
Time limit: 8 hours
Why do it? Generous time limit.
Other Events: Marathon Relay.
Web Site: www.afmarathon.wpafb.af.mil
Phone: (937) 257-4350

Avenue of the Giants (Humboldt, CA)
Date/field size: May/500
Racewalk Awards: No
Time limit: 7 hours
Why do it? Beautiful course among the tallest trees on earth.
Other Events: 10K
Web Site: www.humboldt1.com/~avenue
Phone: (707) 443-1226

Bermuda Walk-Only Marathon
Date/field size: November/1,200
Racewalk Awards: No.
Time limit: No time limit
Why do it? No runners, no time-limit and it's Bermuda. That does it for me! Course is two loops of the island, starting and finishing in downtown Hamilton. A bit incomprehensible why they don't offer racewalk awards in a walk-only marathon though!
Other Events: Half-marathon
E-mail: brooks@cul.net
Phone: (407) 758-0755

Catalina Island (California) Marathon
Date/field size: March
Racewalk Awards: No
Time limit: No time limit
Why do it? For the scenery. The boat ride out to the island is worth doing a marathon for!
Other Events: None
Web Site: www.goracenet.com
Phone: (714) 978-1528

Canadian International Marathon (Toronto)
Date/field size: October/3,700
Racewalk Awards: No
Time limit: 5 hours, but walkers start 2 hours early.
Why do it? It's a first-class marathon in one of the world's great cities.
Other Events: ½ Marathon and Marathon Relay.
Web Site: www.runtoronto.com
Phone: (416) 972-1062

Country Music Marathon (Nashville, TN)
Date/field size: April/16,000 including several thousand walkers.
Racewalk Awards: No
Time limit: 8 hours
Why do it? Live country music all along the course and a headliner act afterwards. And there are lots and lots of walkers.
Other Events: No other races, but there is always a concert by a major act following the race, in addition to the 26 bands that play at every mile mark of the marathon.
Web Site: www.cmmarathon.com
Phone: (615) 880-1058

Dublin (Ireland) Marathon
Date/field size: Late October/3,500
Racewalk Awards: No
Time limit: 9 ½ hours
Why do it? Course runs through Dublin's historic Georgian streets and passes Phoenix Park. Major charity team (Leukemia, Arthritis, Diabetes) marathon destination.
Other Events: Kids' "Minithon."
Web Site: www.internet-ireland.ie/dublin-marathon
Phone: (353) 1676-4647

Fletcher Challenge (Rotorura, New Zealand)
Date/field size: May/2,300
Racewalk Awards: No
Time limit: 7 ½ hours
Why do it? The Fletcher Challenge is the largest and most prestigious road race in New Zealand. Rotorura is the main tourist center in New Zealand, and the center of Maori culture. The course circles Lake Rotorura.
Other Events: None
Web Site: www.nz.com/rotorura/sport/fletcher/index.htm
Phone: (64) 7348 8448

Fox Cities Marathon (Appleton, WI)
Date/field size: October/1,500
Racewalk Awards: No
Time limit: 6 hours
Why do it? The Fox Cities marathon course winds through seven Wisconsin communities along the Fox River, crossing seven bridges decorated for the marathon.
Other Events: Marathon Relay, 2.62 –Mile Run/Walk, Kids' 400-Meter Run.

Web Site: www.altcom.com/foxcitiesmarathon
Phone: (414) 830-7259

Gold Coast Marathon (Southport, Queensland, Australia)
Date/field size: July/2,500
Racewalk Awards: No
Time limit: 8 ½ hours
Why do it? The Gold Coast is known as Australia's "Vacation Playground," featuring shopping, rainforests and access to the Great Barrier Reef.
Other Events: Half-Marathon, 10K Walk
Web Site: www.goldcoastmarathon.com.au
Phone: (61) 7 5527 1363

Kilauea Volcano Marathon (Kilauea, HI)
Date/field size: July/1,000
Racewalk Awards: No
Time limit: 8 hours
Why do it? The lava-trail course starts in the desert surrounding the volcano and climbs through rain forests to the summit. Not an easy course, so even good runners wind up walking a lot of the race.
Other Events: 10-Mile Crater Rim Run and 5-Mile Caldera Walk.
Web Site: www.bishopmuseum.org/vac/rimrun.html
Phone: (808) 982-7783

Lincoln (Nebraska) All-Sport Marathon
Date/field size: May/1,500
Racewalk Awards: No
Time limit: 6 ½ hours (walkers start 90 minutes early.)
Why do it? Walkers get an early start and an escort by Lincoln Track Club cyclists. The scenic course passes by Folsom Zoo and several parks and golf courses, and goes around Holmes Lake.
Other Events: Half-Marathon.
Web Site: www.lincolnrun.org/marathon.htm
Phone: (402) 435-3504

Madison (Wisconsin) Marathon
Date/field size: May/3,500
Racewalk Awards: No
Time limit: 6 ½ hours
Why do it? A beautiful course along Lake Mendota, and finishing in Olin Park on Lake Monona.
Other Events: Half-Marathon, Marathon Relay, 10K, 5K Walk.

Web Site: www.madison-marathon.com
Phone: (608) 256-9922

Marathon des Chateaux du Medoc (Paullic, France)
Date/field size: September/Limited to 10,000 entrants (Apply early!).
Racewalk Awards: No
Time limit: 6:15—sort of.
Why do it? The course runs through 53 of the world's most famous vineyards in the Medoc region north of Bordeaux. Marathoners are encouraged to wear outrageous costumes in the race, and—*mon Dieu!*—wine is served at every mile mark!
Other Events: Recuperation Outing and Wine Tasting.
Web Site: www.marathondumedoc.com
Phone: 33 (0) 5 56 59 1720 or (800) 444-4097

Maui Marathon
Date/field size: October/2,500 limit (Apply out early!)
Racewalk Awards: No
Time limit: 8 hours
Why do it? The Maui Marathon is another no-brainer. According to the marathon web site: "A major part of the course runs within 50 feet of the Pacific Ocean where humpback whales can be seen playing in the cobalt blue waters..." Enough said. Bet the farm it's going to be hot and humid though.
Other Events: 5K Fun Run.
Web Site: www.mauimarathon.com
Phone: (808) 871-6441

Mayor's Midnight Sun Marathon (Anchorage, AK)
Date/field size: Late June/4,500 with about 1,000 walkers
Racewalk Awards: No
Time limit: 9 hours
Why do it? A great excuse to visit the 49th state; cool, usually dry weather; walkers start an hour early, so there's actually a very generous 9-hour limit for walkers. One of the Leukemia & Lymphoma Society's biggest event marathons. The course starts and finishes on paved roads and bike paths, but there is an 8-mile section on hilly, dirt military tank trails.
Other Events: Half-Marathon, 5-Miler, Youth "Run-A-Round."
Web Site: www.ci.anchorage.ak.us
Phone: (907) 343-4474

Melbourne (Australia) Marathon
Date/field size: October/6,000

Racewalk Awards: No
Time limit: 6 ½ hours
Why do it? Lots of entertainment and great crowds all along the course.
Other Events: Half-Marathon, 6K Fun Walk, Marathon Bike Tour.
Web Site: None
Phone: (61) 39 819 6888

Mid-South Marathon
Date/field size: November/200 runners, 15 racewalkers.
Racewalk Awards: Check web site. Possibly.
Time limit: 6 hours. Early start possible if desired.
Why do it? Very supportive race director. Scenic small-town course.
Other Events: Half-marathon.
Web Site: www.midsouthmarathon.com
Phone: (870)238-5528

New York City Marathon
Date/field size: November/30,000, with several thousand walkers and runner/walkers.
Racewalk Awards: No. Racewalk division dropped in 1997.
Time limit: 10 hours
Why do it? It's New York! Broadway, 5th Avenue, Central Park; the course winds through all five boroughs of New York; 2 million spectators and dozens of bands line the route. Definitely one of the most exciting races on the planet.
Other Events: International Breakfast Run (5K) the day before the marathon.
Web Site: www.nycmarathon.org
Phone: (212) 423-2249

Official All Star Café Myrtle Beach (South Carolina) Marathon
Date/field size: February/3,000
Racewalk Awards: No
Time limit: 8 hours
Why do it? Small field, flat course, scenic views of the Atlantic Ocean. Live entertainment and All Star Café festivities. Proceeds benefit Leukemia & Lymphoma Society.
Other Events: Marathon Relay.
Web Site: www.coastal.edu/mbmarathon
Phone: (803) 349-2733

Philadelphia Marathon
Date/field size: November/4,000
Racewalk Awards: No

Time limit: None
Why do it? The course goes through Independence National ﹍﹍
passes the U.S. Mint, Benjamin Franklin's grave, Betsy Ross House,
Philadelphia Zoo and finishes at the Philadelphia Museum of Art. (Charge up
the Museum steps *a la* Rocky Balboa optional.)
Other Events: Broad Street Run.
Web Site: www.philadelphiamarathon.com
Phone: (215) 686-0054

Rock & Roll Marathons (San Diego, Phoenix)
Date/field size: May or June (San Diego), January (Phoenix)/20,000 including
several thousand walkers.
Racewalk Awards: No
Time limit: 7 hours
Why do it? The music; lots of walkers.
Other Events: No other races, but there is always a concert by a major act
following the race, in addition to the 26 bands that play at every mile mark.
Web Site: www.rnrmarathon.com, www.rnraz.com
Phone: (858) 450-6510

Twin Cities Marathon (Minneapolis-St. Paul, MN)
Date/field size: October/Limited to 7,000
Racewalk Awards: No
Time limit: 6 hours
Why do it? Among the best crowds anywhere; fast course, cool weather and a
great expo.
Other Events: 5-Mile Run, 1-Mile Celebrity Run, ½ Mile Kids' Run.
Web Site: www.doitsports.com/marathons/twincities
Phone: (612) 673-0778

Vancouver International Marathon (Canada)
Date/field size: May/5,000
Racewalk Awards: No
Time limit: None. Finish line stays open until the last walkers finish, but
participants may have to move to sidewalks after 6 hours.
Why do it? Mostly flat, scenic course through Vancouver's scenic ocean
waterfront and lush parkland with views of snowcapped mountains.
Other Events: Half-marathon and 5K Run/Walk
Web Site: www.wi.bc.ca
Phone: (604) 872-2928

Walt Disney World Marathon (Orlando, FL)
Date/field size: January/10,000 with about 100 racewalkers
Racewalk Awards: Some years. Three-deep awards for overall men and women, as well as in 10-year age groups from 39-under to 70+.
Time limit: 7 hours, but slower walkers permitted to start early.
Why do it? Mickey Mouse starts the race with a fireworks display; great Mickey finishers' medallions; course winds all through the Magic Kingdom.
Other Events: Half-Marathon, "Family Fun" 5K.
Web Site: Yes, but the address changes constantly! Search for Disney Marathon at google.com.
Phone: (407) 939-7810

Duke City, First Light, Honolulu, Jersey Shore, Lake Tahoe and **Portland**, outlined in the previous racewalking section, are all great "People's" marathons that encourage walk participants. For a very good up to date list of walker-friendly and racewalk marathons, go to www.marathonwalking.com/marathon_calendar.htm.

Other interesting events

Bataan Memorial Death March (White Sands, NM)
Date/field size: April/2,000
Racewalk Awards: Sort of. Not a judged racewalk, but there are categories for civilians and military personnel "marchers." Military must wear combat boots and backpacks weighing a minimum of 35 pounds. There are also team awards.
Time limit: None
Why do it? Definitely not your typical marathon. Commemorates the Bataan Death March following the surrender of Bataan, Philippines on April 9, 1942. Prisoners were forced to march 65 miles without food and water.
Other Events: None
Web Site: http://members.aol.com/bcmfofnmz/memorialmarch.html

Bermuda End-to-End Charity Walk
Date/field size: May/2,000
Racewalk Awards: No
Time limit: None
Why do it? Location, location, location. This 26-mile non-competitive walk starts in St. Georges, passes through Hamilton and ends at Dockyard on the other side of the island.
Other Events: 15-mile Middle-to-End Walk from Hamilton to Dockyard.
E-mail: ete@ibl.bm
Phone: (441) 299-8885

Big Sur (California) 21-Mile "Powerwalk"
Date/field size: April/Limited to 500 in the 21-mile walk. (3,000 in the marathon run)
Racewalk Awards: No, but ceramic medallions to all finishers
Time limit: 5 ½ hours
Why do it? Marathons don't get more scenic. Walkers treated very well.
Other Events: Big Sur Marathon, Marathon Relay, and 5K. Walking clinic at race expo.
Web Site: www.bsim.org/marathon
Phone: (408) 625-6226

Capetown (South Africa) Big Walk
Date/field size: October/30,000 walkers
Racewalk awards: Yes, for males and females in many age groups.
Time limit: No
Why do it? Started in 1903, the Capetown Big Walk is the biggest timed walk event in the world. Medals and certificates for all finishers in 80K, 50K, 36K, 25K, 20K, 18K, 13K, 11K, 10K and 9K races.
Web Site: www.bigwalk.co.za
Phone: 021-6830913

Discovery Walk Festival (Vancouver, WA)
Date/field size: April/1,100
Racewalk Awards: No
Time limit: No time limit
Why do it? Non-competitive event, but it's one of the few walker-only marathons around.
Other Events: 5K, 10K, half-marathon, 20-mile, and marathon events
Web Site: www.discoverywalk.org
Phone: (800) 222-8733

Victoria (British Columbia) International Blossom Walk
Date/field size: April/800
Racewalk Awards: No.
Time limit: None
Why do it? If you want to do a marathon but don't want to be bullied by runners, this and other "volkssport" marathons are for you!
Other Events: 5K, 10K and 20K walks
Web Site: www.coastnet.com/~blossom/main.htm
Phone: (250) 361-0266

Appendix II

Marathon Pace Chart

Mile	5K	5 Miles	10K	15K	10 Miles	20K	½ Mar.
8:00	24:51	40:00	49:43	1:14:34	1:20:00	1:39:25	1:44:53
8:15	25:38	41:15	51:16	1:16:54	1:22:30	1:42:32	1:48:09
8:30	26:24	42:30	52:49	1:19:13	1:25:00	1:45:38	1:51:26
8:45	27:11	43:45	54:22	1:21:33	1:27:30	1:48:44	1:54:42
9:00	27:58	45:00	55:55	1:23:53	1:30:00	1:51:51	1:57:59
9:15	28:44	46:15	57:29	1:26:13	1:32:30	1:54:57	2:01:16
9:30	29:31	47:30	59:02	1:28:33	1:35:00	1:58:04	2:04:32
9:45	30:18	48:45	1:00:36	1:30:53	1:37:30	2:01:10	2:07:49
10:00	31:04	50:00	1:02:08	1:33:12	1:40:00	2:04:16	2:11:06
10:15	31:51	51:15	1:03:42	1:35:32	1:42:30	2:07:23	2:14:22
10:30	32:37	52:30	1:05:14	1:37:52	1:45:00	2:10:29	2:17:39
10:45	33:24	53:45	1:06:48	1:40:12	1:47:30	2:13:35	2:20:56
11:00	34:10	55:00	1:08:20	1:42:32	1:50:00	2:16:42	2:24:12
11:15	34:57	56:15	1:09:54	1:44:52	1:52:30	2:19:48	2:27:29
11:30	35:44	57:30	1:11:28	1:47:11	1:55:00	2:22:55	2:30:45
11:45	36:30	58:45	1:13:00	1:49:31	1:57:30	2:26:01	2:34:02
12:00	37:17	1:00:00	1:14:34	1:51:51	2:00:00	2:29:08	2:37:19
12:15	38:04	1:01:15	1:16:08	1:54:11	2:02:30	2:32:14	2:40:36
12:30	38:50	1:02:30	1:17:40	1:56:31	2:05:00	2:35:20	2:43:52
12:45	39:37	1:03:45	1:19:14	1:58:51	2:07:30	2:38:27	2:47:08
13:00	40:24	1:05:00	1:20:48	2:01:10	2:10:00	2:41:34	2:50:25
13:15	41:10	1:06:15	1:22:20	2:03:30	2:12:30	2:44:40	2:53:42
13:30	41:57	1:07:30	1:23:54	2:05:50	2:15:00	2:47:46	2:56:58
13:45	42:43	1:08:45	1:25:26	2:08:10	2:17:30	2:50:53	3:00:15
14:00	43:30	1:10:00	1:27:00	2:10:30	2:20:00	2:54:00	3:03:31
14:15	44:16	1:11:15	1:28:32	2:12:50	2:22:30	2:57:06	3:06:47
14:30	45:03	1:12:30	1:30:06	2:15:09	2:25:00	3:00:12	3:10:04
14:45	45:50	1:13:45	1:31:40	2:17:29	2:27:30	3:03:19	3:13:21
15:00	46:36	1:15:00	1:33:12	2:19:49	2:30:00	3:06:25	3:16:38
15:15	47:23	1:16:15	1:34:46	2:22:09	2:32:30	3:09:31	3:19:55
15:30	48:10	1:17:30	1:36:20	2:24:29	2:35:00	3:12:37	3:23:11
15:45	48:56	1:18:45	1:37:52	2:26:49	2:37:30	3:15:43	3:26:28
16:00	49:42	1:20:00	1:39:24	2:29:08	2:40:00	3:18:50	3:29:44
16:15	50:29	1:21:15	1:40:59	2:31:28	2:42:30	3:21:57	3:33:01
16:30	51:16	1:22:30	1:42:32	2:33:48	2:45:00	3:25:04	3:36:18
16:45	52:03	1:23:45	1:44:06	2:36:08	2:47:30	3:28:10	3:39:34
17:00	52:48	1:25:00	1:45:36	2:38:28	2:50:00	3:31:16	3:42:50
17:15	53:36	1:26:15	1:47:12	2:40:48	2:52:30	3:34:23	3:46:07
17:30	54:22	1:27:30	1:48:44	2:43:07	2:55:00	3:37:29	3:49:24
17:45	55:09	1:28:45	1:50:18	2:45:27	2:57:30	3:40:36	3:52:41
18:00	55:54	1:30:00	1:51:48	2:47:47	3:00:00	3:43:42	3:55:58
18:15	56:42	1:31:15	1:53:24	2:50:07	3:02:30	3:46:48	3:59:15
18:30	57:29	1:32:30	1:54:59	2:52:27	3:05:00	3:49:54	4:02:31
18:45	58:15	1:33:45	1:56:30	2:54:47	3:07:30	3:53:00	4:05:48
19:00	59:02	1:35:00	1:58:04	2:57:06	3:10:00	3:56:07	4:09:05
19:15	59:49	1:36:15	1:59:39	2:59:26	3:12:30	3:59:14	4:12:21
19:30	1:00:35	1:37:30	2:01:10	3:01:46	3:15:00	4:02:20	4:15:38
19:45	1:01:22	1:38:45	2:02:44	3:04:06	3:17:30	4:05:28	4:18:55
20:00	1:02:08	1:40:00	2:04:16	3:06:25	3:20:00	4:08:32	4:22:11

Conversions:

1 mile = 1,609.1 meters
1 kilometer = .6214 miles
5K = 3.107 miles
10K = 6.214 miles
15K = 9.321 miles

20K = 12.428 miles
25K = 15.535 miles
30K = 18.642 miles
35K = 21.749 miles
40K = 24.856 miles

Marathon = 42.195 kilometers = 26 miles, 385 yards

15 Miles	25K	30K	20 Miles	35K	40K	Marathon	50K
2:00:00	2:04:16	2:29:08	2:40:00	2:54:00	3:18:50	3:29:45	4:08:32
2:03:45	2:08:09	2:33:47	2:45:00	2:59:26	3:25:04	3:36:18	4:16:18
2:07:30	2:12:02	2:38:27	2:50:00	3:04:52	3:31:16	3:42:52	4:24:04
2:11:15	2:15:55	2:43:07	2:55:00	3:10:18	3:37:28	3:49:25	4:31:50
2:15:00	2:19:49	2:47:46	3:00:00	3:15:44	3:43:42	3:55:58	4:39:38
2:18:45	2:23:42	2:52:26	3:05:00	3:21:10	3:49:54	4:02:31	4:47:24
2:22:30	2:27:35	2:57:05	3:10:00	3:26:36	3:56:08	4:09:05	4:55:10
2:26:15	2:31:28	3:01:45	3:15:00	3:32:02	4:02:20	4:15:38	5:02:56
2:30:00	2:35:21	3:06:25	3:20:00	3:37:29	4:08:32	4:22:11	5:10:42
2:33:45	2:39:14	3:11:04	3:25:00	3:42:55	4:14:45	4:28:46	5:18:28
2:37:30	2:43:07	3:15:44	3:30:00	3:48:21	4:20:58	4:35:18	5:26:14
2:41:15	2:47:00	3:20:23	3:35:00	3:53:47	4:27:10	4:41:51	5:34:00
2:45:00	2:50:53	3:25:03	3:40:00	3:59:14	4:33:22	4:48:25	5:41:46
2:48:45	2:54:46	3:29:42	3:45:00	4:04:40	4:39:36	4:54:58	5:49:32
2:52:30	2:58:39	3:34:22	3:50:00	4:10:06	4:45:50	5:01:32	5:57:18
2:56:15	3:02:32	3:39:01	3:55:00	4:15:32	4:52:03	5:08:05	6:05:04
3:00:00	3:06:25	3:43:42	4:00:00	4:20:58	4:58:16	5:14:38	6:12:50
3:03:45	3:10:18	3:48:22	4:05:00	4:26:24	5:04:29	5:21:11	6:20:36
3:07:30	3:14:11	3:53:02	4:10:00	4:31:51	5:10:42	5:27:45	6:28:22
3:11:15	3:18:04	3:57:41	4:15:00	4:37:17	5:16:55	5:34:18	6:34:08
3:15:00	3:21:57	4:02:21	4:20:00	4:42:44	5:23:08	5:40:51	6:43:55
3:18:45	3:25:50	4:07:00	4:25:00	4:48:10	5:29:21	5:47:24	6:51:40
3:22:30	3:29:43	4:11:40	4:30:00	4:53:37	5:35:34	5:53:58	6:59:26
3:26:15	3:33:36	4:15:20	4:35:00	4:59:03	5:41:47	6:00:31	7:07:12
3:30:00	3:37:29	4:20:59	4:40:00	5:04:29	5:47:59	6:07:05	7:14:59
3:33:45	3:41:22	4:25:39	4:45:00	5:09:56	5:54:12	6:13:38	7:22:44
3:37:30	3:45:15	4:30:19	4:50:00	5:15:22	6:00:25	6:20:11	7:30:30
3:41:15	3:49:08	4:34:59	4:55:00	5:20:48	6:06:38	6:26:44	7:38:16
3:45:00	3:53:02	4:39:38	5:00:00	5:26:14	6:12:50	6:33:18	7:46:03
3:48:45	3:56:55	4:44:17	5:05:00	5:31:40	6:19:03	6:39:51	7:53:48
3:52:30	4:00:48	4:48:57	5:10:00	5:37:07	6:25:16	6:46:24	8:01:34
3:56:15	4:04:41	4:53:37	5:15:00	5:42:33	6:31:29	6:52:57	8:09:20
4:00:00	4:08:34	4:58:16	5:20:00	5:47:59	6:37:42	6:59:31	8:17:07
4:03:45	4:12:27	6:02:56	5:25:00	5:53:26	6:43:55	7:06:04	8:26:52
4:07:30	4:16:20	6:07:36	5:30:00	5:58:52	6:50:08	7:12:38	8:34:38
4:11:15	4:20:13	6:12:15	5:35:00	6:04:18	6:56:21	7:19:11	8:42:24
4:15:00	4:24:06	5:16:55	5:40:00	6:09:44	7:02:33	7:25:44	8:48:11
4:18:45	4:27:59	5:21:35	5:45:00	6:15:10	7:08:46	7:32:17	8:55:56
4:22:30	4:31:52	5:26:14	5:50:00	6:20:36	7:14:59	7:38:51	9:03:42
4:26:15	4:35:45	5:30:54	5:55:00	6:26:03	7:21:12	7:45:24	9:11:28
4:30:00	4:39:38	5:35:33	6:00:00	6:31:29	7:27:25	7:51:57	9:19:16
4:33:45	4:43:31	5:40:13	6:05:00	6:36:55	7:33:38	7:58:30	9:27:00
4:37:30	4:47:24	5:44:53	6:10:00	6:42:21	7:39:51	8:05:03	9:34:46
4:41:15	4:51:17	5:49:32	6:15:00	6:47:47	7:46:04	8:11:36	9:42:32
4:45:00	4:55:10	5:54:12	6:20:00	6:53:14	7:52:16	8:18:09	9:50:20
4:48:45	4:59:03	5:58:52	6:25:00	6:58:40	7:58:29	8:24:43	9:58:04
4:52:30	5:02:56	6:03:31	6:30:00	7:04:06	8:04:42	8:31:16	10:05:50
4:56:15	5:06:49	6:08:11	6:35:00	7:09:32	8:10:54	8:37:49	10:13:36
5:00:00	5:10:42	6:12:50	6:40:00	7:14:59	8:17:07	8:44:22	10:21:24

Resources

Clubs and organizations

AIMS (Association of International Marathons and Road Races)
The Association of International Marathons and Road Races was established in London in May 1982 to foster and promote marathoning and road racing throughout the world. AIMS standards of course measurement have been recognized and adopted by the International Amateur Athletics Federation. Most major marathons are AIMS members and have AIMS-certified courses.

AIMS
Hugh Jones, Secretary
10 Theed Street, Suite 3
London SE1 8ST
England
www.aims-association.org

American Volkssport Association
A volksmarch is a non-competitive walk you do with a club, your family, your pet or all by yourself. Volksmarching got its name from its origins in Europe. Today there are thousands of volkssport clubs around the world, allied in the International Volkssport Federation, the IVV.

American Volkssport Association
1001 Pat Booker Road, Suite 101
Universal City, TX 78148
(800) 830-WALK
avahq@aol.com
www.ava.org

Dave's World Class Racewalking
I conduct one or two week-long racewalking camps and 15 to 18 weekend clinics per year in cities throughout the U.S. For a clinic schedule or information on how to host a clinic in your hometown, write or visit the clinic information board on my World Class web site.

World Class Racewalking
43 W. Hathaway Rd.
Mobile, AL 36608
www.racewalking.org
DMcG@Racewalking.org

National Organization of Mall Walkers
More than 1,000 malls across the U.S. support official mall walking clubs. The National Organization of Mall Walkers can help you find a mall-walking club in your area, or help you to charter your own.

National Organization of Mall Walkers
P.O. Box 191
Hermann, MO 65041
(573) 486-3945

North American Racewalking Foundation (NARF)
Founded in 1986 by Elaine Ward to promote Racewalking in the United States and Canada the Foundation provides information on how to find a club or coach, how to start a club, how to become a certified racewalk judge, and just about anything else related to the sport. The organization also sells a number of books and videos on technique and training, including the *How to Walk Faster—Tips from the Pros* video and the *Fast Walking Technique and Training* manual.

North American Racewalking Foundation
P.O. Box 50312
Pasadena, CA 91115-0312
(818) 577-2264
NARWF@aol.com

190

Partnership for a Walkable America

The partnership's mission is to increase awareness of the healthful benefits of walking and to increase the safety and accessibility of sidewalks and pedestrian pathways for walking in communities throughout the United States.

National Safety Council

1121 Spring Lake Drive
Itasca, IL 60143-3201
(630) 285-1121
www.nsc.org

Road Runners Club of America

The Road Runners Club of America is the national association of not-for-profit running clubs dedicated to promoting long distance running as a competitive sport and healthful exercise. They have traditionally been very open to the needs of walkers in running races like marathons.

Road Runners Club of America

1150 S. Washington Street, Suite 250
Alexandria, VA 22314
(703) 836-0558
execdir@rrca.org

TOPS (Take Off Pounds Sensibly), Inc.

TOPS is a nonprofit organization founded in 1948 to help people to loose weight through sensible dieting, exercise, and positive reinforcement. In 1997 TOPS launched the largest ongoing community-based walking program in the US.

TOPS

4575 S. Fifth Street
P.O. Box 07360
Milwaukee, WI 53207-0360
(414) 482-4620
www.tops.org

Walkers Club of America

Founded in 1911, the oldest and foremost walking organization in the United States. The club is primarily an informational organization that promotes walking for competition and exercise, organizes walking events, publishes a quarterly newsletter, conducts seminars and instructional camps, offers instructional certification and assistance in starting your own club. For more information write to WCA:

Walkers Club of America
Howard Jacobson, Executive Director
Box 640
Levittown, NY 11756
www.walkamerica.org
CoachJak@pouch.com

YMCA of the USA

The "Y" is a good place to find information on walking clubs, and a great place to treadmill walk, pool walk, weight train.

YMCA of the USA
101 N. Wacker Drive
Chicago, IL 60606
(312) 977-0031
www.ymca.net

Magazines

Marathon & Beyond
411 Park Lane Drive
Champaign, IL 61820
(217) 359-9345
www.marathonandbeyond.com

Ohio Racewalker
Jack Mortland, Editor

3184 Summit Street
Columbus, OH 43202

Prevention Magazine
33 E. Minor Street
Emmaus, PA 18098
(610) 967-5171
www.prevention.com

Shape Magazine
21110 Irwin Street
Woodland Hills, CA 91367
(818) 884-6800
www.shapeonline.com

Marathon training teams

American Diabetes Association's Team Diabetes
The American Diabetes Association's mission is to prevent and cure diabetes and to improve the lives of all people with diabetes. Team Diabetes is the American Diabetes Association's marathon training program. Participants receive an 18- to 20-week personalized training program, coaching, group workouts and travel to one of the world's most famous marathons.

American Diabetes Association
1701 North Beauregard Street
Alexandria, VA 22311
(888) DIABETES
www.diabetes.org

Arthritis Foundation's Joints in Motion Training Team
Joints in Motion is a marathon training/fundraising event benefiting the Arthritis Foundation. Participants receive an 18- to 20-week training schedule, round-trip airfare and hotel accommodations to walk a major international marathon.

National Arthritis Foundation
1330 West Peachtree Street
Atlanta, GA 30309
(800) 960-7682
www.arthritis.org

Fred's Team
Shortly after New York City Marathon Race Director Fred Lebow's death from cancer on October 9, 1994, the New York Road Runners Club and the Memorial Sloan-Kettering Cancer Center in New York City, where Lebow was treated, announced the formation of "Fred's Team." The marathon training team's goal is to raise $1.5 million to endow the Fred Lebow Chair in Neuro-Oncology at Sloan-Kettering, which has been rated the nation's number one cancer center seven years in a row by U.S. News & World Report.

Memorial Sloan-Kettering Cancer Center
1275 York Avenue
New York, NY 10021
(800) 876-7522
www.mskcc.org

Leukemia & Lymphoma Society of America's Team in Training
Team in Training is the original and the largest charity marathon training program in the country. You'll be provided with a qualified coach who will train you to go the distance, training partners for weekly group workouts, and an all-expense-paid trip to a marathon in exotic locales like Anchorage, Bermuda, Honolulu or London, in exchange for helping to raise money for the Leukemia Society. For information on a chapter in your area call:

Team in Training
(800) 482-TEAM
www.lsa-teamintraining.org

Marathon Strides against Multiple Sclerosis
The National Multiple Sclerosis Society's marathon training program and team.

The National Multiple Sclerosis Society
733 Third Avenue, New York, NY 10017
(800) Fight-MS
www.nmss.org

National AIDS Marathon Training Team
6-month training program developed by Jeff Galloway to help participants complete a marathon to raise money for AIDS research.

National AIDS Marathon Training Program
PO Box 38797
Los Angeles, CA 90038-0797
(323) 993-1400
www.aidsmarathon.com

Women Walk the Marathon
A training program and support group for women who are planning to walk the Portland Marathon. Long group walks and monthly lectures are held in Portland, Eugene and Vancouver, OR.

Women Walk the Marathon
5319 SW Westgate Drive, Suite 131
Portland, OR 97721-2430
(503) 292-6929
www.spiritone.com/~nwwalk

Walking product retailers

Eastbay
PO Box 8066
Wausau, WI 54402-8066
(800) 826-2205
www.eastbay.com

Hoy's Sports
1632 Haight Street
San Francisco, CA 94117
(415) 252-5370

(800) 873-4329
www.hoys.com

North American Racewalking Foundation (NARF)
P.O. Box 50312
Pasadena, CA 91115-0312
(818) 577-2264
NARWF@aol.com

RaceReady Clothing
(800) 537-6868
www.raceready.com

Road Runner Sports
5549 Copley Drive
San Diego, CA 92111
(800) 453-5443
www.roadrunnersports.com

Sports & More
8097 Hwy. 59 South
Foley, AL 36535
(800) 397-5480

Title Nine Sports
5743 Landragan Street
Emeryville, CA 94608
(800) 609-0092
thefolks@title9sports.com
www.title9sports.com

Walking product manufacturers

adidas
P.O. Box 4015
Beaverton, OR 97076-4015
(503) 972-2300
www.adidas.com

Asics
Attn: Consumer Relations
10540 Talbert Avenue
Fountain Valley, CA 92708
(800) 678-9435
consumer@asicstiger.com
www.asicstiger.com

CamelBak Products, Inc.
1310 Redwood Way
Suite 200
Petaluma, CA 94954
(800) 767-8725
www.camelbak.com

Champion (JogBra)
5 New England Drive
Essex, VT 05452
(888) 301-5151
www.championforwomen.com

Hersey Custom Shoe Company
63 Hersey Lane
Wilton, Maine 04294
www.herseycustomshoe.com/comp.html

New Balance Athletic Shoes & Apparel
61 N. Beacon Street
Boston, Ma 02134
(800) NBF-STOR
www.newbalance.com

Nike
One Bowerman Drive
Beaverton, OR 97005
(800) 806-6453
www.nike.com

Polar Heart Rate Monitors
370 Crossways Park Drive
Woodbury, NY 11797-2050
(800) 227-1314
www.polar.usa.com

Prostretch
P.O. Box 680728
San Antonio, TX 78268
(800) 535-3629
www.prostretch.com

Reebok International Ltd.
1895 J. W. Foster Blvd.
Canton, MA 02021
(888) 898-9028
www.reebok.com

Saucony
13 Centennial Drive
Peabody, MA 01961
(800) 365-4933
www.saucony.com

Walking Web Sites

About.com Walking
www.walking.about.com

Dave's Worldclass Racewalking
www.racewalking.org

Racewalk.com
www.racewalk.com

Walkertown USA
www.walkertownusa.com

The Walking Connection
www.walkingconnection.com

Women.com Walking Clubs
www.women.com/clubs/walking.html

Aerobic metabolism The creation of energy through the combustion of carbohydrates and fats in the presence of oxygen.

Adenosine triphosphate (ATP) The primary fuel used by our bodies when exercising. Fats and carbohydrates are broken down into ATP in the muscles.

AIMS   (Association of International Marathons and Road Races). A "trade group" for marathon race directors that promotes, markets, and ensures standardized courses for marathons throughout the world.

Anaerobic metabolism The creation of energy through the combustion of carbohydrates in the absence of oxygen.

Bursa Closed, fluid-filled sacs that prevent tendons from rubbing directly against bones.

Bursitis Painful inflammation of an overused bursa.

Capillaries   The body's smallest blood vessels. Capillaries directly supply the muscles with oxygenated blood, and remove carbon dioxide, lactate and other wastes.

Carbohydrate loading The process of ingesting a higher than normal percentage of carbohydrates to induce the muscles to store more glycogen before a marathon or long walk.

Cardiac drift The tendency for heart rate to rise gradually throughout a workout due to dehydration and rising temperature within the muscles.

Center of gravity An imaginary point that would exist if you crushed your body down to a single, centrally located point. In humans, this point lies behind, and just below, the navel.

ChampionChip A small electronic transmitter that walkers and runners wear on their shoes during a marathon. The chip relays each athlete's position on the course to provide accurate finish times and to ensure that everyone completes the entire course.

Cross-training Training in activities other than walking or racewalking, to improve fitness without over-taxing the walking muscles.

Detraining The loss of fitness that occurs after a prolonged break from training.

Economy A measure of how efficiently an athlete utilizes oxygen when exercising. An economical walker is able to walk fast while working at a relatively low percentage of his or her VO_2 max.

Economy repeats Bursts of short, fast walking, interspersed with long rest intervals. Economy repeats teach a walker to walk efficiently at high speed.

Effective stride length The amount of stride length behind a walker's body. A walker should attempt to maximize stride length behind the body, and limit the length of the stride in front of the body.

Ergogenic aids A legal or illegal substance ingested by an athlete to potentially increase athletic performance.

Fartlek Swedish for "speed play." Workouts where a walker accelerates and decelerates randomly throughout the workout.

Fast-twitch muscle fibers Muscle fibers that produce energy "glycolytically," by breaking down glycogen in the absence of oxygen. They produce rapid contractions, but create lactic acid as a by-product. Some fast-twitch fibers are convertible to non-lactate producing slow-twitch fibers.

General Adaptation Syndrome (GAS) Describes the process of improving fitness by stressing the body, then allowing it to recover from and adapt to that stress.

Glycogen Carbohydrate stored in the liver and muscles. Glycogen is used as a fuel during exercise.

Glycolysis The creation of energy through the intra-muscular combustion of glycogen.

IAAF (International Amateur Athletics Federation). The world governing body of track and field, road racing and racewalking.

Lactic Acid Also referred to as "lactate." Lactic acid is a by-product of anaerobic glycolysis that inhibits muscular contractions.

Lactate threshold Also known as *anaerobic threshold*, is the point at which lactate begins to increase in the muscles and blood faster than it can be broken down.

Lactate threshold intervals Near-race pace intervals of 400 meters to 5 kilometers in duration with short rests between each, used to "teach" a walker's muscles to produce energy aerobically, without creating lactic acid as a by-product.

Lebow, Fred Creator and long-time race director of the New York City Marathon.

Louis, Spiridon Winner of the first Olympic marathon in 1896.

Maximum heart rate (MHR) The highest number of times a walker's heart can beat in a minute of exercising. Maximum heart rate is a genetically determined "random" variable; it has no bearing on a walker's current fitness or potential as an athlete.

Mitochondria The "powerhouses" of the cells. Mitochondria produce the energy that produces muscle contractions.

Negative splits Covering the second half of a marathon (or any given distance) faster than the first half.

Palpation Manual exploration of any body part, but in our case poking around your muscles and tendons with your fingers looking for "knots" and adhesions.

Pheidippides Allegedly the world's first marathoner. Greek messenger said to have run from Marathon to Athens only to fall dead at the end of his run. Maybe he should have walked?

Resting heart rate (RHR) The number of times a walker's heart beats per minute while at complete rest. Resting heart rate will decrease as the walker's heart becomes larger and stronger with training. A low resting heart rate is an indicator of fitness.

Singlet A sleeveless mesh tank top worn by many marathon walkers.

Slow-twitch muscle fibers Muscle fibers that produce energy by converting fats into energy aerobically. They are not able to contract as quickly as fast twitch fibers, but they do not produce lactic acid as a by-product.

Split times Intermediate times for a workout or race. Most walkers will want to keep track of how fast they walk each mile or 5K "split" of their marathons.

Tempo training A type of sustained lactate threshold training that approaches a walker's race pace and race distance. Steady-state tempo workouts are walked at a continuous pace; acceleration tempo workouts are walked at an ever-increasing pace.

VO_2 max A measure of the maximum amount of oxygen that a walker can take in and process during exercise. It is measured in milliliters of oxygen per kilogram of body mass per minute. It is *one* measure of a walker's athletic potential.

VO_2 max intervals *Very* fast 400- to 1,600-meter repeats with long rest intervals between each, used by walkers to increase their ability to take in and process large volumes of oxygen while walking at high speeds.

REFERENCES

Benyo, Richard, editor. *Marathon & Beyond, Volume 1, Issue 1,* Human Kinetics Press, Champaign, IL, 1997.

Bompa, Tudor. "Peaking for the Major Competitions, Parts I and II," *Science Periodical on Research and Technology in Sport,* April and May, 1984.

Clippinger-Robertson, Karen. "Abdominal Strength for Race Walkers," unpublished, 1986.

Clippinger-Robertson, Karen. "Flexibility for Race Walkers," unpublished, 1986.

Cooper, Pamela. *The American Marathon,* Syracuse University Press, Syracuse, NY, 1999.

Craythorn, Dennis, and Rich Hanna. The Ultimate Guide to International Marathons, Marathon Publishers, Inc., Sacramento, CA, 1998.

Edwards, Sally. *The Heart Rate Monitor Book,* Polar, CIC, Port Washington, NY, 1994.

Fenton, Mark, and Dave McGovern. *Precision Walking,* Polar Electro, Port Washington, NY, 1995.

Galloway, Jeff. *Galloway's Book on Running,* Shelter Publications, Inc., Bolinas, CA, 1984.

Hauman, Riël. *Century of the Marathon 1896-1996,* Human & Rousseau, Capetown, South Africa, 1996.

Henderson, Joe. The Complete *Marathoner,* World Publications, Inc., Mountain View, CA, 1978.

Henderson, Joe. *Marathon Training,* Human Kinetics, Champaign, IL, 1997.

Higdon, Hal. *Marathon: The Ultimate Training and Racing Guide,* Rodale Press, Emmaus, PA, 1993.

Hilliard, Craig. "Weight Training and Conditioning for Walkers," *Modern Athlete and Coach,* Vol. 29:2, April 1991, pp. 36-38.

Jacobson, Howard. *Racewalk to Fitness,* Walkers Club of America Press, New York, NY, 1980.

Maher, Peter. *World Marathon Guide,* Marathon Sports Marketing, Inc., St. Petersburg, FL, 1998.

Martin, David E., Ph.D. and Peter N. Coe. *Better Training for Distance Runners,* Human Kinetics Press, Champaign, IL, 1997.

McGovern, Dave. *The Complete Guide to Racewalking Technique and Training,* World Class Publications, Mobile, AL, 1998.

Meyers, Casey. *Walking: A Complete Guide to the Complete Exercise,* Random House, New York, NY, 1992.

Neporent, Liz, M.A. *Fitness Walking for Dummies,* IDG Books Worldwide, Inc., Foster City, CA, 2000.

Noakes, Tim, M.D. *Lore of Running,* Leisure Press, Champaign, IL, 1991.

Olan, Ben, ed. *Pursuit of Excellence: The Olympic Story,* The Associated Press and Grolier, Danbury, CT, 1979.

Rudow, Martin. *Advanced Racewalking,* Technique Publications, Seattle, WA, 1987.

Salvage, Jeff and Westerfield, Gary. *Walk Like an Athlete,* Salvage Writes Publications, Marlton, NJ, 1996.

Sheehan, Dr. George. *Dr. Sheehan on Running,* Bantam Books, New York, NY, 1975.

Temple, Cliff. *The Marathon Made Easier,* Atheneum Press, New York, NY, 1982.

ABOUT THE AUTHOR

Dave McGovern is a champion marathon walker and coach. Winner of the competitive racewalk divisions of the New York, Los Angeles, Honolulu Disney, Mardi Gras, First Light and Mississippi marathons, Dave has a personal-best marathon walk time of 3:38:42. A racewalk coach since 1986 and a Leukemia & Lymphoma Society "Team in Training" marathon coach since 1997, Dave has prepared his beginning marathon walkers to compete in the Anchorage, Bermuda, Chicago, Country Music, Disney World, Rock & Roll, and Vancouver marathons and has yet to have a walker fail to complete the distance.

A member of the U.S. National Racewalk Team and a 12-time National Champion at all distances from 10 to 40 kilometers, Dave's personal-best time of 1:24:29 ranks him as the 5th fastest 20-kilometer walker in U.S. history. Dave is a USA Track & Field and Leukemia Society of America certified coach, and the coach of the Olympic racewalkers of Ghana and the Fiji Islands. He's taught thousands to racewalk faster and more legally, with fewer injuries, through his "Dave's World Class" week-long training camps and weekend clinics. The author of *The Complete Guide to Racewalking Technique and Training* and *Precision Walking*, and a writer for *Walking* magazine, Dave is a rare individual: A first-rate coach and athlete, able to communicate his ideas in a witty, easy-to-understand style.